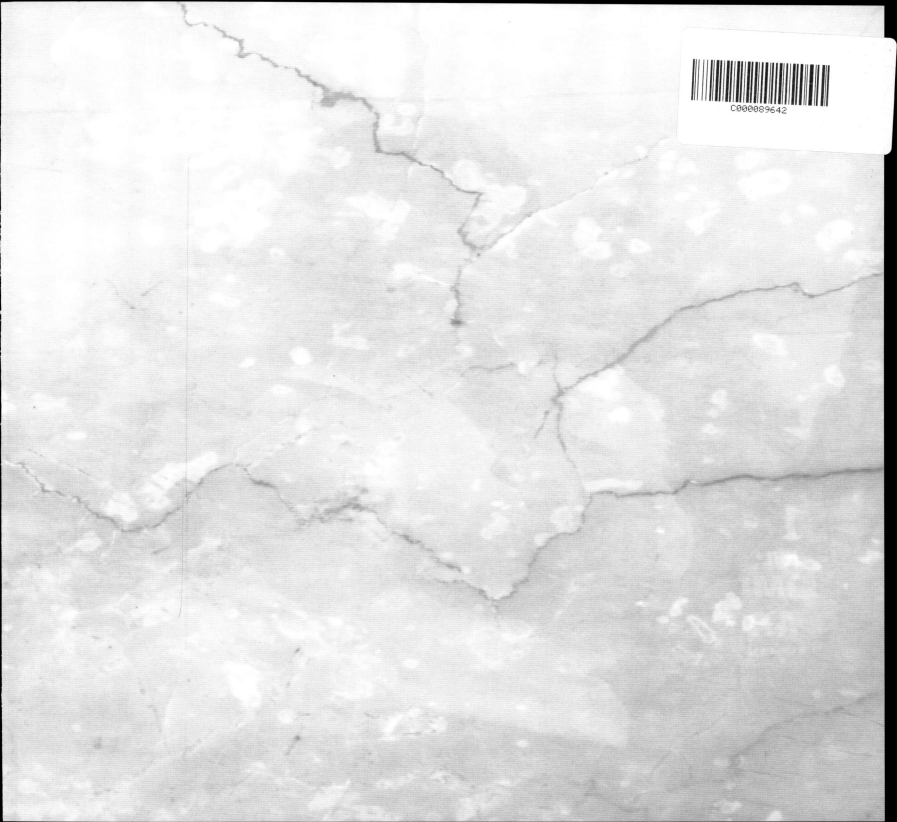

# Jubilee 2012

## CELEBRATIONS & TOURS

Text copyright: Rex Publications Ltd
Pictures: Press Association Images; Nadia Huggins (page 19);
Government of the British Virgin Islands (page 51);
UK in Mozambique (page 60); UK in Uganda (page 202);
Commonwealth Youth Programme Regional Centre
for Africa (page 203).
Design copyright: Mpress (Media) Ltd
Editor: Joe Little

ISBN: 978- 0- 9572559- 5- 1

Published By:
Rex Publications Ltd
64 Charlotte Street
London W1T 4QD
Telephone: 020 7436 4006
Fax: 020 7436 3458
www.majestymagazine.com

Designed and Printed by m press
Unit Four, Ashton Gate, Harold Hill, Romford, RM3 8UF Tel: 01708 379 777

# Contents

FOREWORD by JOE LITTLE,
Managing Editor of *Majesty* magazine

WHAT AN INCREDIBLE year 2012 has been. In Britain we've had the excitement of the Olympic and Paralympic Games but, more importantly to royal aficionados like you and me, this has been the year in which we – and millions of people around the world – celebrated the Diamond Jubilee of Her Majesty Queen Elizabeth II.

I well remember the tabloid media predictions in the months preceding the Queen's Silver Jubilee celebrations in 1977 – and indeed her Golden Jubilee a quarter of a century later. The public just aren't interested, we were told, so why bother to organise events that no one will attend?

How wrong those prophecies proved to be. More than a million people took to the streets of London on each ceremonial occasion to demonstrate their respect and love for the woman who, in 1947, at the then tender age of 21, declared that 'my whole life whether it be long or short shall be devoted to your service'.

The public response was equally magnificent in 2012. Despite some truly atrocious weather at times – particularly when the Thames River Pageant was taking place – the British, and many foreign visitors too, turned out in force with their flags to greet the Queen and the Duke of Edinburgh wherever they went in the United Kingdom.

Members of the royal family have travelled extensively overseas on the Queen's behalf throughout her Diamond Jubilee year, visiting all the realms and territories, Commonwealth countries and Crown Dependencies. As many of these engagements as possible have been included in *Jubilee 2012: Celebrations & Tours*, our record of a royal year quite unlike any other.

'Memories of all this year's happy events will brighten our lives for years to come,' the Queen said in a televised message, but for her and her family there have been anxious times too, notably when Prince Philip was taken ill. And as a grandmother, she understandably worries about Prince Harry since his return to the conflict in Afghanistan, even though he went with her blessing. Such is life, royal or otherwise.

Like the Queen, we continue to look forward. So what next for Her Majesty? In June 2013 she will commemorate the 60th anniversary of her coronation, another regal milestone. Then, in September 2015, comes one of the most significant moments in royal history: the point at which Queen Elizabeth II, at the age of 89, becomes the longest-reigning British monarch. That month she will overtake Queen Victoria, her great-great-grandmother, who reigned for 63 years and 216 days.

The Queen is healthy, happy and glorious; long may she reign over us.

# Sixty Glorious Years

## By JOE LITTLE

IT'S EARLY FEBRUARY and a large group of people are standing in a field in a bleak part of the Sandringham estate. They could be forgiven for thinking they are in Siberia as it's bitterly cold, but nevertheless all are delighted to be there. Three days before the 60th anniversary of her accession, the Queen is coming to plant an English oak, one of six million native trees in the Woodland Trust's project to create 60 special 'Diamond Woods' and hundreds of smaller 'Jubilee Woods' across Britain.

Her Majesty arrives in a Land Rover accompanied by the Princess Royal, and with only a scarf around their heads for protection both royal women seem impervious to the freezing temperature. The required handshakes and introductions out of the way, the Queen deftly places three shovelfuls of soil around the tree roots, with a 'there we are' as if confirmation were needed that the job is done. How many trees has the monarch planted in the last six decades must be a question on the minds of onlookers right now.

Princess Anne, as the trust's patron, makes a brief but eloquent speech in which she talks about this being a well-established royal tradition and recalls growing up alongside an avenue of trees elsewhere on the estate that had been planted to mark her mother's coronation in 1953.

**The Queen views a display by the children of Dersingham Infant and Nursery School**

**FROM FAR LEFT: The Queen and the Princess Royal arrive at the site of the new Diamond Jubilee Wood**

**Her Majesty plants an oak tree on 3 February, the start of the Sandringham Diamond Jubilee Wood**

**The monarch seems oblivious to the winter chill as she meets the organisers and local schoolchildren**

The royal ladies then meet a group of enthusiastic children from Flitcham and Sandringham & West Newton schools. In all, 150 youngsters would spend the day planting more than 500 trees on the Sandringham estate. The Queen's Diamond Jubilee celebrations really have begun.

More often than not, on the last weekend of the Queen's winter break in Norfolk she attends a Sunday morning service at the church of St Peter and St Paul in the village of West Newton and afterwards presents prizes in the nearby hall for children's church attendance.

This year was no exception, despite the considerable amount of snow that had fallen overnight. But thanks to the many hands who helped clear the approach road and church path, the Queen and the Duke of Edinburgh arrived bang on time.

After a 40-minute service conducted by the Reverend Jonathan Riviere, Her Majesty received flowers from children gathered at the church gate.

Oliver Bassham, 7, was first in the queue. Having handed the monarch a bunch of flowers, he then produced a bag of Werther's Original caramels. She seemed uncertain whether to take them or not until Oliver explained: 'They're not for you. They're for Prince Philip.'

**CLOCKWISE FROM LEFT: The royal couple with the Reverend Jonathan Riviere at West Newton**

**Prince Philip inspects the packet of sweets presented to him after the service**

**The Queen speaks to well-wishers as she walks to the nearby village hall**

**Her Majesty is presented with flowers and other gifts by members of the public**

The Queen, putting on a mock expression of surprise, smiled as she turned to her 90-year-old husband, saying: 'I think these are for you.'

'Oliver just thought it would be nice to give Prince Philip something as the Queen always gets flowers at church,' said Oliver's mother. 'My husband works at Sandringham and he knows that Prince Philip likes his toffees so we got him some.'

The Duke had been due to travel to nearby King's Lynn to participate in the local Royal British Legion branch's 90th anniversary parade, but the event was cancelled because of the snow.

At the beginning of a year of celebration and reflection, the Queen issued a Diamond Jubilee message:

'Today, as I mark 60 years as your Queen, I am writing to thank you for the wonderful support and encouragement that you have given to me and Prince Philip over these years and to tell you how deeply moved we have been to receive so many kind messages about the Diamond Jubilee.

'In this special year, as I dedicate myself anew to your service, I hope we will all be reminded of the power of togetherness and the convening strength of family, friendship and good neighbourliness, examples of which I have been fortunate to see throughout my reign and which my family and I look forward to seeing in many forms as we travel throughout the United Kingdom and the wider Commonwealth.

'I hope also that this Jubilee year will be a time to give thanks for the great advances that have been made since 1952 and to look forward to the future with clear head and warm heart as we join together in our celebrations.

'I send my sincere good wishes to you all.'

Elizabeth R

**The King's Troop Royal Horse Artillery fire a 41-gun salute in London's Hyde Park**

The Queen leaves King's Lynn town hall after receiving the loyal address on 6 February

OPPOSITE PAGE:
Her Majesty, having driven to the school in Dersingham, enjoys a show staged by the children in her honour

Three-year-old Isaac Minns plays up to the cameras as the monarch tours the classrooms

On 6 February, the Queen marked the historic milestone in typically modest fashion with a visit to Dersingham Infant and Nursery School on the Sandringham estate. She was treated to a short play, written and performed in her honour by children aged between three and seven, about the changes the country has seen during her reign.

'It's a wonderful opportunity for the children to share the Queen's special day and celebrate the achievements of the school, and I'm sure it will be remembered by them for many years to come,' said Gayle Platt, the head teacher.

The children, whose parents include Sandringham estate workers, had only been able to rehearse their play for two weeks because the teachers had been sworn to secrecy about the royal visit.

Earlier that morning the Queen visited the 15th-century town hall in King's Lynn, where she viewed displays of photographs and artefacts, including the charter of 1441 granted to the town by Henry VI and the register of her father's birth at Sandringham.

Borough Mayor Colin Sampson accompanied the Queen around the town hall.

'Starting off a year-long worldwide chain of events is really quite something,' he said. 'It has been a huge pleasure and honour.'

Mr Sampson read a loyal address to congratulate the Queen on '60 years of unparalleled service to the nation'. He went on: 'West Norfolk residents are very appreciative of all that Your Majesty has done to support the area and you have earned a very special place in our hearts.'

He gave the Queen a framed copy of the address and in return she signed a newly-released portrait of herself for the town hall.

Although the day's events were distinctly low-key, a Buckingham Palace spokesman said it was unusual for the Queen to carry out any public engagements at all on the anniversary of her accession, as it is also the anniversary of her father's death.

A 41-gun salute by the King's Troop Royal Horse Artillery in London's Hyde Park marked the accession anniversary. It was followed by a 62-gun salute at the Tower of London and there was also a 21-gun royal salute at Edinburgh Castle.

The Queen, with Hugo Vickers, Chairman of the Jubilee Walkway Trust, prepares to unveil the Jubilee Greenway disc

# February

ON 29 FEBRUARY the Queen, accompanied by the Duke of Edinburgh and the Duke of Gloucester, officially unveiled the first Jubilee Greenway disc outside Buckingham Palace. It forms part of a symbolic 60km walking and cycling route from the palace through Hyde Park, to Kensington, connecting Paddington along the Regent's Canal through Victoria Park to the Olympic Park.

It then passes along Bazalgette's Greenway and down through Beckton District Park to the Thames. The route crosses the river to Woolwich and returns along the Thames Path to Tower Bridge where it joins the Queen's Walk and goes back to Buckingham Palace.

Two weeks earlier, the Queen and Prince Philip attended the first public event to mark her Diamond Jubilee, a multi-faith reception at Lambeth Palace. They were received by the Archbishop of Canterbury, Dr Rowan Williams, and Mrs Williams.

Representatives of the eight non-Christian religions – Baha'i, Buddhist, Hindu, Jain, Sikh, Jewish, Muslim and Zoroastrian – were presented to the royal couple, who later went on to meet Christian representatives.

**CLOCKWISE FROM RIGHT: The Queen with the Archbishop of Canterbury at Lambeth Palace on 15 February**

**Buddhist guests at the multi-faith reception pray after showing the monarch a silver stupa**

**Cardinal Cormac Murphy-O'Connor, Archbishop Emeritus of Westminster, is presented to Her Majesty**

The Queen, Supreme Governor of the Church of England, in her address highlighted the importance of faith in society and the 'critical guidance' it offered in life.

'The concept of our established Church is occasionally misunderstood and, I believe, commonly under-appreciated. Its role is not to defend Anglicanism to the exclusion of other religions. Instead, the Church has a duty to protect the free practice of all faiths in this country.'

The Church was 'woven into the fabric of this country' and had helped to build a better society,' the Queen added.

It has 'created an environment for other faith communities and indeed people of no faith to live freely,' she went on. 'Our religions provide critical guidance for the way we live our lives and for the way in which we treat each other.

'Here at Lambeth Palace we should remind ourselves of the significant position of the Church of England in our nation's life.'

The Queen said the occasion marked an opportunity to reflect on the importance of faith in 'creating and sustaining communities' across Britain. 'Faith plays a key role in the identity of many millions of people, providing not only a system of belief but also a sense of belonging,' she continued.

Dr Williams paid tribute to the Queen's 'personal commitment' to her office as a call from God, which he said was 'at the heart of her understanding of her role'.

**LEFT: The Countess of Wessex visits St Lucia School of Music during a Diamond Jubilee tour of the West Indies with her husband in February**

**Prince Harry dances with Chantol Dormer during a visit to the Rise Life project in Jamaica on 6 March**

# On Her Majesty's Service

## By CAMILLA TOMINEY, royal editor of the *Sunday Express*

THIS WAS ALWAYS going to be a royal tour with a difference and Prince Harry did not disappoint on his first overseas visit on behalf of the Queen, which was to mark her Diamond Jubilee. Protocol was almost immediately set aside as the 27-year-old Prince's arrival in Belize on 2 March was marked with a colourful street party in the capital, Belmopan. The third-in-line to the throne carried out the formal duty of naming a street Queen Elizabeth II Boulevard in his grandmother's honour before letting his hair down under the Central American stars.

He proved an instant hit with the 2,000-strong crowd as he sampled local food and drink and even performed several impromptu jigs to the sound of the steel drums.

'He's a wonderful dancer. I would give him 10 out of 10,' said dancer Denese Enrique after putting the young royal through his paces. 'He was reluctant at first, saying he would dance a little bit but not too much, but then he really looked like he was enjoying himself.'

Game Harry also enjoyed a traditional Creole dance with Lavern Arau, who thought the Prince was 'great at wiggling his hips'.

The colourful scenes unfolded after Harry, dressed in a *guyabera*, the traditional Belizean shirt, gave a speech hailing his grandmother as an 'inspiration'. Passing on Her Majesty's good wishes, he said: 'She remembers so fondly her visits to this beautiful realm and speaks of the warmth of the welcome she received on her most recent visit in 1994. I'm only sorry she can't make it and you're stuck with me.'

Prince Harry gives a speech as he attends a 'block party' on Queen Elizabeth II Boulevard in Belmopan

Government of Belize

In a nod to screams coming from the sidelines, he joked: 'The noisy corner here; and a bit more noise on this side, please', before declaring in Creole: '*Mek wih go paaty*' ('Let the party begin'), to whoops from the audience.

It was the first of many speeches delivered by Harry showing not only his newfound taste for diplomacy but also his bubbly personality. In Nassau, capital of the Bahamas, he addressed a youth rally at the national stadium, where he joked: 'Don't you look smart!'

He later delivered a more serious speech at the Royal Bahamian Defence Force base at Coral Harbour, where, dressed for the very first time in the tropical No. 1 uniform of the Blues and Royals, his Army regiment, worn with the Army Air Corps beret, he paid tribute to his fellow comrades.

**LEFT: The Prince 'shakes his stuff' with a local woman during his walkabout at the block party**

**BELOW: Harry tries on a mask whilst taking part in another traditional dance**

'I am directed by the Queen, as head of the RBDF, to extend Her Majesty's heartfelt good wishes to you all on the occasion of her Diamond Jubilee,' he said. 'In the past Bahamians have fought and, tragically, some have laid down their lives for their country and the cause of freedom. You are a credit to your nation.'

The most colourful scenes of the 11-day tour came in Jamaica, where Harry proved to be the star attraction on the island. Screaming fans came out in force for a glimpse of the Prince taking in all manner of cultural Caribbean experiences. The crowds were so frenzied in the seaside town of Falmouth, on the north coast, that a walkabout had to be cancelled after the royal party was mobbed on the quayside.

**OPPOSITE PAGE: Prince Harry, wearing Blues and Royals No. 1 tropical dress, attends a Sunday service at Christ Church Cathedral in Nassau, Bahamas**

**BELOW: The royal visitor accepts a portrait of himself from artist Jamaal Rolle during a reception in Rawson Square in Nassau**

The undoubted highlight of his four-day visit to Jamaica came at the Usain Bolt running track at the University of the West Indies in Kingston, where Prince Harry came face to face with running royalty.

Hilarious scenes unfolded as Harry was put through his paces by the world's fastest man ahead of the London 2012 Olympics, where the Prince would act as an ambassador for Team GB along with the Duke and Duchess of Cambridge. As the champion was preparing to race against Harry, the cheeky royal distracted him before making a dash for the finish line, much to the delight of all the onlookers.

The chemistry between the fun-loving pair was palpable as they took part in an unplanned press conference, with Harry joking that he too was in his prime when he was 25, Bolt's age.

A visit to Bustamente Children's Hospital saw Harry fulfil one of his mother's legacies. Diana, Princess of Wales had been due to visit the cardiac unit before her life was tragically cut short in August 1997.

In scenes reminiscent of his mother's charitable work with children, the big-hearted Prince toured the wards taking time to chat with many poorly toddlers. Passing by cots with sleeping babies in them he joked: 'Everyone's sleeping who is due to meet me!'

Harry was given another warm welcome at historic Devon House, when the Most Honourable Portia Simpson Miller, Prime Minster of Jamaica, embraced him in an affectionate bear hug. The move proved all the more surprising after Mrs Simpson Miller had expressed republican sympathies suggesting that the Commonwealth country should cut ties with the Queen as head of state.

The Prince's charm offensive proved so successful that the Prime Minster declared afterwards: 'We are in love with him [Harry]; we love him! He is a wonderful person, such a beautiful person.'

**LEFT: Portia Simpson Miller, Prime Minister of Jamaica, gives Harry the warmest of welcomes when he arrives for lunch at Devon Hall**

**OPPOSITE PAGE: The Prince meets one of the young patients as he tours Bustamente Children's Hospital in Kingston**

Prince Harry embraced the Jamaica spirit at a children's community centre, Rise Life, when he danced to the reggae beat with Rita Marley, widow of the legendary Bob. Mrs Marley presented her new royal dance partner with a scarf that had once belonged to the *No Woman No Cry* singer.

The tour took on a sombre note when Harry learned of the British Army's darkest day for six years before a visit to Up Park Camp military base. The Apache helicopter pilot had been due to take part in a daredevil abseil down the Rappel Tower but changed his plans after learning of the death of six soldiers in Afghanistan.

Captain Wales, as Harry is known, took part in a 'war simulator' and was given the chance to show off the shooting skills he has honed during his six-year Army career. Wearing a combat helmet and military fatigues, blast glasses, knee and elbow pads, he joined soldiers on a 30-metre range and fired the standard-issue M40 rifle at a target.

On a different note, Prince Harry ended his tour as guest of honour at a glamorous 'Jamaica Night' party at the exclusive Sandals Royal Caribbean Hotel in Montego Bay.

He then jetted to Rio de Janeiro to undertake engagements on behalf of the British government in a bid to strengthen trade with Brazil. The Prince took a Union Jack-branded cable car to the top of Sugarloaf Mountain to open a 'Best of British' cultural event and was greeted by a carnival band, samba dancers and crowds chanting his name.

**LEFT: Harry plays touch rugby with children on Rio de Janeiro's Flamengo Beach on 10 March**

**FAR LEFT: The Prince, wearing a paper mask of his brother William, takes part in a Sport Relief Mile**

There were more sporty scenes the next day as Harry – regarded as the world's most eligible bachelor now – ran a Sport Relief Mile and then took part in a rugby coaching session and a volleyball match at Flamengo Beach. Amid incredibly tight security, he later visited the Complexo do Alemao favela, where he witnessed first-hand the effect poverty has on thousands of Brazilians in urban areas.

Not worn out by the gruelling nature of his overseas debut, the Prince still found the energy for a polo match in Campinas, Sao Paulo State. The Sentebale Polo Cup, held in aid of the charity he set up in his mother's memory for the vulnerable children of Lesotho, marked an appropriate end for a trip that fulfilled all its potential and more.

Harry led the Sentebale team to a 6-3 victory and was rewarded with a kiss from Fernanda Motta, one of Brazil's top models.

**OPPOSITE PAGE: Harry is surrounded by a huge security cordon as he tours the Complexo do Alemao favela in a northern suburb of Rio de Janeiro, where he watched a cricket match and visited a clinic**

**BELOW: The Prince captains the Sentebale team for a charity polo match in Campinas, where he is delighted to meet Fernanda Motta, the celebrated Brazilian model, actress and television host**

# Nordic Realms

By RICHARD PALMER, royal correspondent
of the *Daily Express*

The Prince of Wales and the Duchess of Cornwall in
the Bird Room of the Royal Palace in Oslo before an
official dinner, with, *from left*, Princess Astrid, Queen
Sonja, King Harald, Crown Princess Mette-Marit,
Crown Prince Haakon and Princess Märtha Louise

IT WAS A chance to mix business with pleasure for the Prince of Wales
and the Duchess of Cornwall. An eight-day tour of Scandinavia in
March gave them the opportunity to fly the flag for Britain while
catching up with some of their favourite foreign relatives.

They did it with gusto as the royal houses of Britain, Norway, Sweden
and Denmark celebrated the Queen's Diamond Jubilee and marked the
close ties between the four monarchies dating back to Queen Victoria.

For one princess at least, a personal friendship with Camilla was enough
for her to break with royal protocol. As the consort of the future King of
Norway, Crown Princess Mette-Marit is of the same royal rank as Camilla
and therefore has no need to genuflect before her. Not for the first time,
however, she chose to curtsey to the Duchess when she and her husband,
Crown Prince Haakon, met the visiting British royals.

Quite why is not clear, though it is easy to imagine that Camilla, who has suffered her share of criticism over the years after her adulterous affair with Charles, might have provided some friendly advice and sympathy to the Crown Princess.

Mette-Marit, a former commoner, was vilified as a single mother who had been around drug abusers when she started dating Haakon.

The two women certainly appear to share a bond. 'There is no protocol reason for the curtsey. It's just a matter of personal courtesy,' a source close to the Crown Princess said, confirming that Mette-Marit did not usually pay obeisance to women of a similar rank.

Charles and Camilla soon joined King Harald and Queen Sonja, who have given Norway its own royal celebrations this year with their 75th birthdays, but there was a solemn start to the tour.

After the traditional wreath-laying ceremony at Oslo's National Monument, the four of them met survivors of the Utøya massacre.

**OPPOSITE PAGE: The Duchess of Cornwall and Queen Sonja visit Granebo Outdoor Nursery School in Bergen**

**BELOW: The Prince of Wales meets Lars Hjetland, a survivor of the Utøya massacre, at the Nobel Peace Centre in Oslo**

At the Oslo Nobel Peace Centre, they talked to Labour youth league members who were on the island of Utøya for a summer camp on 22 July 2011 when the right-wing extremist Anders Behring Breivik went on a gun rampage that together with a bomb attack on government offices in Oslo earlier that day left 77 people dead.

Survivors told how they still suffered nightmares but had all been back to the place where their friends were massacred.

'You've all been back? It was very brave of you,' Camilla said. 'The most important thing is to be able to talk about it, and talking to each other, between yourselves.'

The mood was lightened that evening at a dinner in Oslo's Royal Palace, when Charles recalled his first visit to Norway, with his parents and sister Princess Anne, in August 1969.

'It was then that I discovered three memorable and endearing things about the Norwegians – first of all that virtually every house seemed to fly the Norwegian flag; secondly, that our anthems are exactly the same and, thirdly, that Norwegians tend to stay up all night during the summer,' the Prince told the 74 guests dining on a menu that included cured moose.

**OPPOSITE PAGE: Prince Charles struggles to get out of the cockpit of a Gripen fighter jet at Arlanda airport, Stockholm**

**BELOW: The Duchess of Cornwall and Queen Silvia of Sweden on a gun deck during their visit to the *Vasa*, the world's last surviving 17th-century ship**

As Camilla watched, wearing one of several Bruce Oldfield outfits she took on the tour, he also raised a laugh by thanking Norwegians for looking after Prince Harry during his training for a polar trek with disabled servicemen in April last year.

'I cannot thank you enough for ensuring my younger son did not contract frostbite – or lose any vital appendages – while he was in Svalbard exactly a year ago, making a television programme about wounded British servicemen walking to the North Pole,' he said.

In Norway's second city, Bergen, the next day the couple braved heavy rain to tour the area, posing for pictures with people wearing masks bearing the faces of members of the British royal family. The heir to the throne even showed off his skills with an axe, standing astride a log to split it, in a workshop in the historic Bryggen area, a UNESCO World Heritage Site.

**OPPOSITE PAGE:** The King and Queen of Sweden, accompanied by their three children and Prince Daniel, give a luncheon for Charles and Camilla at the Royal Palace In Stockholm

**BELOW:** The royal party wear white coats for a visit to an organic mill at Salta Kvarn

Soon they were in Stockholm, where shortly after landing and being greeted by Prince Carl Philip, Charles was back in a hangar squeezing himself into the cockpit of another plane. He was keen to see the Swedish Air Force Gripen fighter jet but climbing out again proved problematic.

It was all action for Charles. He tried his hand at basketball, shooting hoops with young players at the Fryshuset youth centre in Stockholm. He had three goes and missed with each shot. 'I'm too short to do that,' he complained.

When some boys put on a breathtaking display of skateboarding, he jumped nervously when they came near. 'Did that take long to learn? I'm too old,' laughed the Prince.

At a lunch at the palace, there was a chance to chat with King Carl XVI Gustaf and Queen Silvia and to congratulate their elder daughter Crown Princess Victoria and her husband Prince Daniel on the birth in February of their first child, Princess Estelle.

**OPPOSITE PAGE:** The Duchess samples the wares at Elsinore's Brostraede Fløde-is, the oldest ice cream shop in Denmark

**BELOW:** She and Prince Charles meet a group of war veterans outside St Alban's church in Copenhagen

After visits to the historic 17th-century *Vasa* warship and a bakery, where Camilla had a fit of the giggles, the British royals flew to Copenhagen for the final leg of their tour.

Hosted by Queen Margrethe II of Denmark but escorted principally by Crown Prince Frederik and his wife, Crown Princess Mary, they enjoyed some private time before embarking on a series of official engagements that led them on the penultimate day of the tour to the city of Elsinore, site of Hamlet's castle.

Inside Kronborg Castle, they watched the Royal Shakespeare Company overseeing a drama workshop with local students on the Prince of Denmark's lines in the immortal bard's play.

They also toured the old town, where they found kind hearts and cornets in Denmark's oldest ice cream shop, each trying a vanilla cone with raspberry sauce.

The couple stopped to chat to passers-by, including the owner of a tattoo parlour who offered Charles a free tattoo. 'How long would it take?' asked Charles before politely declining the offer. He remains tattoo-free, although Crown Prince Frederik has a shark tattooed on his leg and his nickname, Pingo, on his shoulder. Charles's ancestors, kings Edward VII and George V, helped popularise the fashion with their own indelible ink designs on their skin.

**OPPOSITE PAGE: The receiving line for a state dinner given by Queen Margrethe at Christian VII's Palace at Amalienborg**

**BELOW: The Prince of Wales in conversation with Prince Henrik, the Prince Consort; and the Duchess of Cornwall dazzles in diamonds**

**Soon after the dinner began, a small fire set off alarms and smoke entered the banqueting hall. Guests were not evacuated**

It was left to Camilla to produce the *pièce de résistance* on the final day. The Duchess, a fan of the Danish crime drama *The Killing*, visited the set and met the star of the television series, actress Sofie Grabol, who plays Sarah Lund.

'I'm an addict. I'm so excited by this,' said Camilla, whose husband had told one of the show's executives the day before that it was one of the few programmes the couple could watch together without fighting over the remote control.

The Duchess, who was presented with a cardigan version of Sarah's trademark Faroe Island jumper, was fascinated by a replica revolver used by Grabol and caused chaos on the set by brandishing it menacingly. Crown Princess Mary cowered and dived for cover as Camilla waved the gun around and then turning to a British reporter admitted, with a wicked grin, that she was the murderer. 'It was me all along.'

Charles, meanwhile, was in an old people's home on a housing estate playing *skomager*, a Danish version of pool, with Crown Prince Frederik; as with the basketball, he failed to pot his ball.

Asked what he thought of Charles's efforts, Knud Jacobsen, 91, who was playing when the two Princes joined in, tried to be diplomatic. 'Middling,' he said.

**OPPOSITE PAGE: The Duchess of Cornwall familiarises herself with props on the set of *The Killing*, much to Crown Princess Mary's surprise**

**BELOW LEFT: Camilla is delighted with the Faroe Island cardigan presented to her by actress Sofie Grabol, who has made the knitwear popular again**

**BELOW: The Prince of Wales and Crown Prince Frederik of Denmark enjoy a game of *skomager* at the retirement home in Copenhagen**

The Queen meets young entertainers in De Montfort Square in Leicester on 8 March

OPPOSITE PAGE: Kate collects flowers from members of the public at Leicester Cathedral

# March

**T**HE QUEEN'S DIAMOND JUBILEE tour of the United Kingdom got off to a very encouraging start on 8 March in Leicester, where huge crowds, nine deep in places, turned out to welcome the monarch at each of her engagements. Scenes such as this would be repeated up and down the country in the following four months.

Her Majesty and the Duke of Edinburgh, accompanied by the Duchess of Cambridge for the first time on a royal 'away day', arrived at Leicester railway station on a scheduled service from London. They then travelled to De Montfort University, via De Montfort Square, where in a carnival atmosphere they watched several cultural dances.

Once inside the Hugh Aston building at the university the royal party toured a number of booths highlighting local projects and charities. The Queen and the Duchess of Cambridge then attended a student fashion parade while Prince Philip was shown the Square Mile project, De Montfort University's programme to help improve the local community.

Her Majesty and Their Royal Highnesses then moved on to Leicester Cathedral for a service of Christian worship with participation from other faiths. Lunch was held in the Grand Hall at nearby St Martins House. Afterwards, the royal trio stopped at the Clock Tower in Leicester city centre to witness a performance on a theme of the Holi festival, entitled '60 Colours'. Before she left, the Queen received a Diamond Jubilee gift from city representatives.

**OPPOSITE PAGE: The Queen and the Duchess of Cambridge enjoy the student fashion show at De Montfort University**

**BELOW: The Duke of Gloucester meets children on Main Street, Tortola, on 6 March during his Diamond Jubilee visit to the British Virgin Islands**

The scene in Westminster Hall on 20 March as, *right*,
the Queen replies to addresses from both Houses of
Parliament to mark her Diamond Jubilee

FAR RIGHT: Guests inspect the specially commissioned
stained glass window, a gift from members of the House
of Lords and the House of Commons

Her Majesty speaks with the Archbishop of Canterbury,
Dr Rowan Williams, at the reception after the ceremony

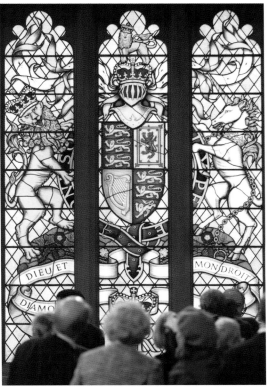

**CLOCKWISE FROM ABOVE:** The opening of MediaCityUK is among Her Majesty's engagements in Greater Manchester on 23 March

The Queen and Prince Philip spend the day in north London on 29 March, visiting Valentine's Park, Redbridge; Waltham Forest Town Hall; and Krishna Avanti School in Harrow (*pictured*)

The Queen receives loyal addresses from 27 'Privileged Bodies', including the University of Oxford, the Greater London Authority (*Boris Johnson pictured*) and the Dean and Chapter of St Paul's Cathedral, at Buckingham Palace on 27 March

# April

THE QUEEN DISTRIBUTED Royal Maundy money to 172 people during a service at York Minster on 5 April. To mark her Diamond Jubilee, the monarch handed out money to people from all 44 of the UK's Christian dioceses; usually, it is given to people from a single diocese.

Thousands of people cheered as the Queen, the Duke of Edinburgh and Princess Beatrice of York arrived for the service. The Dean of York said the minster was honoured to have been chosen to host the service, which was last held in the city in 1972.

This year, 86 women and 86 men – one for each of the Queen's 86 years – received the money in two purses in recognition of their services to the Church and their communities. The red purse contained a small amount of money in lieu of food and clothing.

The white purse contained silver Maundy coins consisting of the same number of pence as the years of the sovereign's age.

Continuing her Diamond Jubilee tour of the United Kingdom, the Queen and Prince Philip visited Wales on 26 and 27 April.

They arrived in Cardiff on the royal train and drove to Llandaff Cathedral for a service celebrating Her Majesty's 60-year reign. More than 600 people attended the service, where the Archbishop of Wales, Dr Barry Morgan, praised the Queen's commitment to public life.

'Over the last 60 years, amidst all the shifting sands of public opinion and different viewpoints, you have regarded the Christian faith as the rock on which you have been able to draw strength and comfort,' he said.

'It is a reminder to the rest of us that this country has been shaped by the Christian faith and that faith is still important in our national life.'

**OPPOSITE PAGE: The Queen, the Duke of Edinburgh and Princess Beatrice after the Royal Maundy service at York Minster on 5 April**

**BELOW: Included with this year's Maundy money is a special £5 coin to mark the Diamond Jubilee**

**ABOVE:** The Queen is presented with two park benches to mark her Diamond Jubilee as she holds a reception for the Royal Engineers Association at Windsor Castle on 18 April

**LEFT:** The Earl of Wessex receives a replica of the Liberty Bell from the Mayor of Philadelphia during his Diamond Jubilee visit to the United States in April

**OPPOSITE PAGE:** The Queen, accompanied by Prince Philip and Lord Stirling, views the royal rowbarge *Gloriana* for the first time on 25 April at Greenland Pier in southeast London

Her Majesty's tour included a meeting with the Grand Slam-winning Welsh rugby squad at Margam Country Park.

After lunch, the Queen and the Duke of Edinburgh moved on to Merthyr to visit Cyfarthfa High School and Cyfarthfa Castle Museum. They also viewed displays by the local Mountain Rescue team, Merthyr Scouts and the Forestry Commission.

On the second day, the monarch paid tribute to the people of Wales for their 'remarkable spirit' and praised their 'fortitude and resilience'. She gave the speech after attending a service at Ebbw Vale's Christ Church and meeting community groups at a reception.

'I have travelled the length and breadth of this country during my 60 years as your Queen,' Her Majesty said.

'Prince Philip and I have shared many of the joys and sadnesses of the Welsh people in that time and have always been struck by your sense of pride and your undimmed optimism.

'That remarkable spirit of Wales has been very evident in this valley today.'

Earlier, the royal couple visited the village of Aberfan, where the Queen opened Ynysowen Community Primary School. Once again, hundreds of well-wishers turned out to greet them.

**CLOCKWISE FROM LEFT: The Prince of Wales meets police officers in Peel, Isle of Man, on 26 April as part of the Queen's Diamond Jubilee tour**

**The Queen and Prince Philip view a rugby-related art exhibition at Margam Country Park**

**Her Majesty shelters from the rain as she visits Cyfarthfa High School in Merthyr**

**Princess Anne is shown a Save the Children project in Mozambique during her Diamond Jubilee visit**

**Flowers for the Queen at the Gwent Archive and Ebbw Vale Works Archive Trust on 27 April**

The Queen and the Duke of Edinburgh prepare to review the Diamond Jubilee national parade of Queen's Scouts at Windsor Castle

RIGHT: Her Majesty is briefed by Bear Grylls (Chief Scout) before the parade on 29 April

FAR RIGHT: The Queen undertakes a walkabout from Windsor Castle to the town's Guildhall on 30 April for a Diamond Jubilee celebration

A total of 144 people, including 116 children, died when a coal waste tip slid down a mountain, engulfing a school and surrounding houses. Since the tragedy in 1966, which all but wiped out an entire generation of the community's school children, the Queen has visited the community on four occasions.

From Ebbw Vale, the royal couple went to Glanusk Park, near Crickhowell, Powys. There they attended 'Diamonds in the Park', a festival of rural activities and sports.

Queen Elizabeth II and her guests pose for a photograph in the Grand Reception Room at Windsor Castle. *Front row, left to right*: Emperor Akihito of Japan, Queen Beatrix of the Netherlands, Queen Margrethe II of Denmark, King Constantine of Greece, King Michael of Romania, The Queen, King Simeon of Bulgaria, the Sultan of Brunei, King Carl XVI Gustaf of Sweden, King Mswati III of Swaziland, and Prince Hans-Adam II of Liechtenstein. *Middle row*: Prince Albert of Monaco, Grand Duke Henri of Luxembourg, King Letsie III of Lesotho, King Albert of the Belgians, King Harald of Norway, the Emir of Qatar, King Abdullah II of Jordan, the King of Bahrain, and the Yang di-Pertuan Agong of Malaysia. *Back row*: Sheikh Nasser Mohammed Al-Jaber Al-Sabah of Kuwait, the Crown Prince of Abu Dhabi, Crown Prince Alexander of Serbia, King George Tupou VI of Tonga, Crown Prince Maha Vajiralongkorn of Thailand, Princess Lalla Meryem of Morocco and Prince Mohammed bin Nawaf bin Abdulaziz Al Saud of Saudi Arabia

# Royal Reunion

## By JOE LITTLE

K INGS, QUEENS, PRINCES and princesses from most of the world's monarchies converged on Windsor Castle on 18 May for a luncheon given by Queen Elizabeth II and the Duke of Edinburgh to mark Her Majesty's Diamond Jubilee. It was quite a gathering.

The royal couple greeted their guests in the Grand Vestibule with affection and good humour before joining them for pre-luncheon drinks in the Waterloo Chamber with 16 members of the British royal family – the Duke and Duchess of Cambridge and Prince Harry among them.

Among the European contingent were King Albert and Queen Paola of the Belgians, Queen Margrethe and Prince Henrik of Denmark, Queen Beatrix of the Netherlands, King Harald and Queen Sonja of Norway, King Carl XVI Gustaf and Queen Silvia of Sweden, Prince Albert and Princess Charlene of Monaco and Prince Hans Adam of Liechtenstein.

Queen Beatrix of the Netherlands is pleased
to meet her British counterpart once again

Queen Elizabeth II receives a kiss from Queen Margrethe II

LEFT: Ninety-year-old King Michael of Romania arrives for the luncheon

Those with considerably further to travel included Emperor Akihito and Empress Michiko of Japan, the Sultan of Brunei, the Yang di-Pertuan Agong and Raja Permaisuri Agong of Malaysia, the Emir of Qatar and Sheikha Mozah, and King Abdullah and Queen Rania of Jordan.

Despite there being so many crowned heads under one roof, it was more of a family get-together than a grand royal event. Indeed many are cousins, to varying degrees, and all were eager to pay tribute to their hostess in her very special year.

Notable absentees were the King and Queen of Spain, whose Golden Wedding anniversary occurred earlier that week without celebration.

It had already been revealed that King Juan Carlos would not travel to Windsor because he was recovering from a broken hip, but almost at the last minute Queen Sofia was ordered to pull out of the luncheon by the Spanish government, which, despite the announcement four months earlier that the Earl and Countess of Wessex would visit Gibraltar in June on behalf of the Queen, made no protest about sovereignty until just days before the high-profile Diamond Jubilee event in Windsor.

Controversy surrounded the invitations extended to the kings of Bahrain and Swaziland because of the poor human rights records in their countries. A Buckingham Palace spokesman said the guest list had been drawn up with the approval of the Foreign Office, and that Britain maintains full diplomatic relations with all of the countries represented at the luncheon.

The Duke and Duchess of Cambridge are at Windsor Castle for his grandmother's Diamond Jubilee lunch

**OPPOSITE PAGE:** Grand Duke Henri and Grand Duchess Maria Teresa of Luxembourg visit the UK for the two-day celebrations

Even the seating plan for the group photograph came in for criticism, with the former kings of Romania and Bulgaria on either side of the Queen, while the Emperor of Japan was, to some observers, relegated to the end of the front row. What people failed to appreciate was that Her Majesty had decided that the monarchs should be arranged in seniority based on their date of accession, which is why King Michael (1927) and King Simeon (1943) were sitting alongside her.

Almost 100 people sat at round tables for up to 12 people in St George's Hall, each table accommodating a sovereign, their spouse (where applicable) and a member of the House of Windsor.

A British-inspired menu was prepared for the royal luncheon using many ingredients sourced locally. To start, guests were given a tartlet of poached egg with English asparagus.

This was followed by a main course of new season Windsor lamb with braised potatoes, artichokes, peas, carrots, broad beans, cabbage, and a tomato and basil salad. Kent strawberries and Vanilla Charlotte concluded the meal, with dessert fruit and cheese also on offer.

**LEFT: The Queen with King Constantine and Queen Anne-Marie of Greece at the pre-lunch reception in the Waterloo Chamber**

**OPPOSITE PAGE: Princess Alexandra is deep in conversation with Emperor Akihito and Empress Michiko of Japan**

The majority of the foreign royal guests were at Buckingham Palace that evening for a black-tie dinner hosted by the Prince of Wales, on behalf of his mother, and the Duchess of Cornwall. The Duke of York, the Earl and Countess of Wessex, the Duke and Duchess of Gloucester, the Duke of Kent, and Prince and Princess Michael of Kent were also present.

Windsor Castle was the venue the next morning for the Armed Forces parade and muster, once again to mark the Diamond Jubilee.

The event began with a 'Diamond Nine' formation flypast of RAF Typhoons and then more than 2,500 Services personnel paraded before the Queen and Prince Philip around the Quadrangle and then through the packed town of Windsor, where the streets were decorated with Union flags, and into Home Park (Private).

Sailors, soldiers and Royal Air Force personnel from nearly all areas of the Armed Forces were represented in the main body of the mile-long parade, together with a tri-Service guard of honour for Her Majesty and six military bands.

**LEFT: The parade of 2,500 men and women from all three Services snakes around the Quadrangle at Windsor Castle**

**OPPOSITE PAGE: The Queen enjoys the impressive sight as sailors, soldiers and RAF personnel march past**

Once the parade had passed, the Queen, who was wearing a turquoise coat and matching hat with purple detail by Angela Kelly, and her husband travelled along the same route to an arena in Home Park (Private) where the troops had mustered for a rousing drumhead service.

Waiting for the royal couple were the Scandinavian monarchs and their consorts, together with the Crown Prince and Crown Princess of Serbia, and the Grand Duke and Grand Duchess of Luxembourg. The Prince of Orange and Princess Máxima were new arrivals but they kept a low profile.

**OPPOSITE PAGE: The Queen, accompanied by the dukes of Edinburgh, Gloucester and Kent, is thrilled and touched by the airborne displays**

**LEFT: The Red Arrows perform a flypast at the end of the Diamond Jubilee Armed Forces muster**

**BELOW: 'Caps – off' is the order as Coldstream Guards give three cheers for Queen Elizabeth II**

There followed a loyal address by General Sir David Richards, Chief of the Defence Staff, who said: 'Her Majesty's support and encouragement over the years has created a very special bond between the monarch and her Forces.'

He went on to acknowledge Prince Philip's service during the Second World War, the Duke of York's involvement in the Falklands conflict and Prince Harry's time in Afghanistan.

'I very much appreciate your kind words,' the Queen said in reply. 'It is a tradition of very long standing that the sovereign, and members of the royal family, are intimately associated with the Armed Forces and have been proud to serve in all three Services.

'In addition, we have special connections with particular commands of the Royal Navy and Royal Marines, corps and regiments of the Army, and air stations of the Royal Air Force. We greatly value these connections as it means we meet the wider family of wives and husbands of the currently serving men and women of the Armed Forces.'

To close the Jubilee celebration, an impressive 78-aircraft flypast from all three Services took place, with helicopters, a Lancaster, Spitfires of the Battle of Britain Memorial Flight, Hawks in an 'E II R' formation and Tucanos in a '60' formation.

The display finished with the world-renowned Red Arrows, much to the delight of Queen Elizabeth II.

**OPPOSITE PAGE:** The Queen views a 90kg cake that took five men at the Defence Food Services School in Hampshire eight weeks to make

**LEFT:** Prince Philip attends a reception after the Diamond Jubilee muster

The Prince of Wales waves to a large crowd
of patriotic well-wishers as he walks along
Prince William Road in Saint John

# For Queen & Country

By LYNNE BELL, *Majesty*'s
Canadian correspondent

THE VISIT TO CANADA in May by the heir to the throne and his wife underscored the country's status as one of the Queen's senior realms and was officially themed 'For Queen and Country: Service to Canada – A Royal and A National Value'. This was inspired by both the Queen's 21st-birthday pledge to the Commonwealth ('I declare before you all that my whole life, whether it be long or short, shall be devoted to your service…') as well as the countless acts of service performed by Canadians in their communities in aid of Crown and country.

The four-day cross-country visit to three provinces – New Brunswick, Ontario and Saskatchewan – by the Prince and the Duchess inevitably began with comparisons to the previous summer's conquest of Canada by the newlywed Duke and Duchess of Cambridge, as well as Charles and Camilla's inaugural and rather low-key visit to Canada as husband and wife in 2009.

However, the senior royal couple soon put the speculation of sceptics to rest as they charmed Canadians from coast to coast with their kindness and courtesy and demonstrated sincere interest in meeting ordinary citizens while celebrating their service, mourning their losses, listening to their concerns and, of course, joining in their celebrations.

The welcome to Canada in the maritime New Brunswick province began with enthusiastic outpourings from crowds at Canadian Forces Base Gagetown, in the town of Oromocto, and in the nearby city of Saint John. The Prince, who in 1975 underwent military training at the base, was presented with a photo album depicting his time there.

Welcomed with full military honours, Charles reminisced: 'I am delighted that my wife and I are beginning this, my 16th, visit to Canada here in Gagetown, where I have fond memories of my own military service as a young naval helicopter pilot in the 1970s at an exercise area in the middle of nowhere which somewhat inaptly took its name from the local town of "Blissville"!

'As the father of two serving sons in the Armed Forces – who seem to have become hereditary helicopter pilots – I am greatly looking forward to talking to members and veterans of Her Majesty's Canadian Armed Forces… and to recognise their particular form of service to the nation.'

Charles and Camilla attend
the official welcome ceremony
at Gagetown Canadian Army
base on 21 May

OPPOSITE PAGE: Local people
make their feelings known to
their distinguished visitors

After fulfilling this promise, culminating with a private meeting with families of the fallen, the Prince and the Duchess made their way to the nearby city of Saint John, also known as the 'Loyalist City'. With an effusive Victoria Day welcome from some 3,000 people – all celebrating the Queen of Canada's official birthday – the city lived up to its reputation.

Here Charles and Camilla echoed elements of the visit to Canada by the Duke and Duchess of Cambridge the previous summer.

They often ran 15 minutes behind schedule in an effort to speak to as many well-wishers (some of them in tears) for as long as possible. Like William and Catherine, they took part in a citizenship ceremony in which a dozen new Canadians (among them people from Wales, the Democratic Republic of Congo and South Korea) were granted Canadian citizenship and posed for photographs with the royal visitors.

At the city's Hazen White-St Francis School, the Prince (like his elder son the summer before) joined in a ball hockey game. But Charles, unlike Prince William, scored a goal and to the cheers of onlookers raised his hockey stick victoriously. The Duchess also joined in the fun when earlier in the day she played the spoons with an Acadian folk group.

Throughout their visit to the school the couple took the excitement of those gathered to meet them in their stride as students, parents and staff surrounded them and seemingly couldn't get enough of them, foreshadowing the next leg of their journey in Toronto.

The couple began their visit to Canada's largest city by performing a feat few Canadians can boast of – celebrating the Victoria Day holiday in two provinces. After the day's festivities in New Brunswick, the couple flew on Royal Canadian Air Force One to Toronto, where that evening they were ferried by an RCMP boat on Lake Ontario to watch a fireworks display with first responders, their families and tens of thousands of Torontonians.

**Watched by his wife, the Prince plays hockey at Hazen White-St Francis School in Saint John**

**RIGHT: Charles is presented with an eagle's feather as he meets First Nation chiefs at the Royal York Hotel in Toronto**

**The Duchess of Cornwall unveils a painting of herself by Richard Stone while visiting the Queen's Own Rifles of Canada in Toronto**

**OPPOSITE PAGE: Camilla with twins Grace and Helena Jordan, aged 7, born on the day she married the Prince of Wales, at the Governor-General's office in Toronto**

The following day, the couple defied any doubters as Toronto residents – like those in New Brunswick – gathered to greet them warmly wherever they went. Their packed schedule had the couple officially meeting a cross-section of Canadian society, among them various dignitaries, Queen Elizabeth II Diamond Jubilee Medal recipients, military veterans, First Nations chiefs, university students, homeless youth, chief executives of Canadian companies and Olympic athletes.

While in Toronto, the Duchess marked some important firsts. As Colonel-in-Chief of the Queen's Own Rifles of Canada – her only Canadian regiment – she made her first speech on Canadian soil.

The Prince of Wales inspects a guard of honour at the military muster at Fort York in Toronto

OPPOSITE PAGE: Charles learns how to scratch and fade with a turntable during a tour of an employment skills workshop in Toronto

Addressing her troops, Camilla said: 'I feel deeply honoured to be standing here today… following in the footsteps of the late Queen Mary and Princess Alexandra.' Then, referring to her military and her Canadian connections, she added, 'As the daughter of a highly decorated World War II hero, and the great-great-great-granddaughter of a Canadian Prime Minister, Sir Alan MacNab… I feel very much a part of your regimental family.'

Before leaving Toronto, the couple reunited as the Prince's seven Canadian regiments and the Duchess's regiment came together for a stirring military muster at which Prime Minister Stephen Harper and his wife, Laureen, were also present.

The Prince of Wales and the Duchess of Cornwall stand in front of a mock train carriage, from which the Queen appears to wave at them, at an exhibition at Government House in Regina

OPPOSITE PAGE: Hewitt Murch receives the Queen's Diamond Jubilee Medal from Charles at Regina's Provincial Legislature

After a cross-country evening flight to the prairie province of Saskatchewan, the couple continued their packed schedule in the capital city of Regina, also known as 'The Queen City'.

At the Legislature, the Prince presented Queen Elizabeth II Diamond Jubilee Medals to worthy recipients just as he had done in New Brunswick and Ontario. To mark the building's centenary, Charles presented the Legislative Assembly with a personally selected piece of oak from the Duchy of Cornwall with which to make a new Black Rod.

In his speech, he said: 'I am particularly proud to present you with a block of oak grown in Duchy of Cornwall woodlands as a lasting reminder of my family's deep affection for this province and her people,' before adding, 'It is indeed a chip off the old block!'

At a different type of Saskatchewan ceremonial, the royal couple partook of First Nations traditions at Regina's First Nations University. Welcomed by traditional drumming and dancing, they moved beyond clichés as they spent time learning about – and in the Prince's case aiding – the futures of First Nations youth.

The royal couple greet performers as they leave Regina's Aboriginal University

OPPOSITE PAGE: Camilla meets children wearing crowns at Government House in Regina

One student, Brad Bellegarde, who dedicated a rap song to Charles and Camilla, said, 'The royal couple coming here is so significant and not just because of the treaties between First Nations peoples and the Crown. They also understand that, for us, "Education is the new buffalo" means that in the past we used every part of the buffalo for our needs. Now, education will provide that for us, and they seem to understand that.'

Charles and Camilla's last Canadian engagement was a performance by the Regina Symphony Orchestra, of which the Prince is patron. At the concert, which took place at the Royal Canadian Mounted Police Training Academy, he was presented with a saddlecloth and appointed Honorary Commissioner of the RCMP by the Prime Minister. The Queen, as sovereign, became commissioner-in-chief.

In spite of all the ceremonial, the couple continued to impress Canadians with their warmth and sincerity. On leaving the concert, guest Shirley McCarron witnessed the Duchess of Cornwall 'backtrack about 12 feet in the rain to talk with an elderly lady who had been waiting for her. I think Camilla is a kind person and I'm sure the Prince has a soft spot for Saskatchewan.'

As they bid farewell to Canada, the Prince of Wales said, 'My wife and I take with us today your countless good wishes and congratulations for the Queen. I shall deliver them with pride on my return to London.'

Judging by the reception they received, the Prince and the Duchess also had good reason to be proud.

# May

MAY WAS A very busy month for the Queen and the Duke of Edinburgh. On 1 May they began a two-day visit to the South West of England in Sherborne, where they arrived on the royal train.

The royal couple drove to Sherborne Abbey. Outside the abbey, they visited a Mad Hatter's Tea Party attended by local schoolchildren. The Queen was shown around a food fair and met People's Millions award winners, whilst Prince Philip went inside Sherborne Abbey and viewed an exhibition of the work of local artisans. Afterwards they went on to Digby Memorial Hall in Sherborne for a 1952 coffee morning event with guests and staff from residential homes in Dorset.

The Queen and Prince Philip then continued by train to Salisbury. They visited the Rifles Regimental Museum and attended a luncheon as guests of Wiltshire and Swindon Council.

In the afternoon they went to Salisbury Cathedral. On arrival in Cathedral Close they saw Wiltshire communities' medieval themed exhibits and entertainment before going inside the cathedral to watch schoolchildren at work on Magna Carta projects.

The Queen and the Duke arrived at Yeovil Pen Mill railway station at the start of the second day of their South-West tour. They went by car to Ninesprings Country Park in Yeovil, where they visited a Diamond Jubilee Country Fayre.

The royal couple were then driven to Crewkerne, where in the town hall they were shown displays of local produce, and also significant historical items and documents.

**RIGHT: A huge crowd is waiting for the Queen in Ninesprings Country Park in Yeovil on 2 May**

**LEFT: Her Majesty is delighted by the welcome she and the Duke of Edinburgh are given**

PLEASE NOTE
All rubbish must be
removed from site
as we do not have
an external bin area.

They arrived in Exeter by helicopter and did a walkabout on Princesshay in the city centre. The Queen later opened the Forum Centre at Exeter University, and afterwards she and Prince Philip were entertained to luncheon at the university. Guests were drawn from Devon and Cornwall.

Meanwhile, the Duke of York was in India between 30 April and 6 May to represent the Queen in the year of her Diamond Jubilee.

By 15 May Her Majesty's Diamond Jubilee tour of the United Kingdom had reached the London boroughs of Bromley, Merton and Richmond.

The Queen and Prince Philip arrived at Queen's Gardens in Bromley to tour a 'London as a Global Centre of Fashion' display in fashion-themed 'domes' and meet London-based designers.

The royal couple subsequently met guests attending the 'Jubilee Road Street Party'. Inside the Glades Shopping Centre, they were shown the winning outfits designed for them by primary schoolchildren, and fashion displays created by art students and designers.

Afterwards, the Queen and the Duke attended a 'British Picnic' themed reception at St Mark's Church of England Academy in Mitcham.

**LEFT: This patriotic four-legged trio in Sherborne seem unimpressed by the Queen's presence**

**OPPOSITE PAGE FROM LEFT: Prince Andrew tries block printing at a children's home near Kolkata**

**The Duke of York tours the Officers' Training Academy in Chennai on 4 May**

**Her Majesty encounters Alice at the Mad Hatter's Tea Party outside Sherborne Abbey**

LEFT: The Queen with some young admirers in Bromley on 15 May

BELOW: Her Majesty meets one of the guests at the Jubilee Road Street Party

OPPOSITE PAGE FROM FAR LEFT: The Queen is given a bracelet by Rose Kimanzi, from the Kenyan contingent, during a tea party at Windsor Castle on 11 May for the Diamond Jubilee Pageant cast

A hug for Her Majesty from an orphan in the Watoto Children's Choir from Uganda

The Queen and Prince Philip arrive at the Diamond Jubilee Pageant in Windsor

In the marquee the royal party met groups of 'achievers' from the 13 south London boroughs. They also saw the 'Chef's Adopt a School' tasting session before having lunch in the assembly hall with more 'achievers'.

The Queen and the Duke of Edinburgh that afternoon visited the 'Wild London' festival in Richmond Park, celebrating the woodlands, parks and gardens of the capital. Princess Alexandra, who has a home in the park, was also present.

While touring the muddy grounds, the Queen was serenaded by the choir of the Chapel Royal at Hampton Court Palace singing 'Now is the Month of May'.

Sir David Attenborough, a special adviser for the event, said she was amused by the song choice given the inclement conditions, and remarked: 'How can they sing with their tongues in their cheeks?'

**ABOVE:** The Queen, the Duke of Edinburgh and the Prince of Wales on the barge *Pride of Sefton* on the Leeds and Liverpool Canal in Burnley, Lancashire, on 16 May

**RIGHT:** Her Majesty watches a parade from the Accrington town hall balcony later that day

**FAR RIGHT:** The monarch travels on the monorail during her visit to Chester Zoo

Students from the Royal Ballet School, which is based at White Lodge, the former royal home in Richmond Park, later treated the distinguished visitors to an excerpt from 'Swan Lake'. Afterwards, the royal party took afternoon tea in Holly Lodge Gardens. Before leaving, the Queen met young and adult riders from Riding for the Disabled.

The Queen and Prince Philip were in Lancashire on 16 May where, accompanied by the Prince of Wales, they travelled on a canal barge and attended the Prince's Charities Regeneration Summit at Burnley College. That afternoon the couple visited the town hall and Victorian market hall in Accrington.

The following morning the Queen and Prince Philip visited Chester Zoo and then Orford Jubilee Park in Warrington, where the sovereign unveiled a sculpture while her husband buried a time capsule.

Before lunch, the Queen and the Duke of Edinburgh went on a brief 'driveabout' in the State Range Rover from Canada Boulevard in Liverpool to Merseyside Maritime Museum, where they boarded a yellow Duckmarine boat and were taken on a short tour by boat around Albert Dock.

**CLOCKWISE FROM ABOVE:** The Queen visits the Royal Academy of Arts in London on 23 May to present Diamond Jubilee Awards to those who have made a special contribution to national culture

**LEFT:** Among the artists, musicians and awards' benefactors that Her Majesty meets while touring the galleries are Sir Paul McCartney and Sandie Shaw, and, *above left*, Joan Collins, Dame Shirley Bassey and Kate O'Mara

# And, They're Off

By INGRID SEWARD,
editor-in-chief of *Majesty*

T HE QUEEN MARKED the start of the four-day Diamond Jubilee Weekend by indulging in her greatest passion – horse racing – on Epsom Downs. Her Majesty and the Duke of Edinburgh were given an affectionate welcome by a crowd of more than 130,000 Derby Day race-goers as they were driven along the straight to the winning post on 2 June – the 59th anniversary of her coronation.

The Duke of York, Princesses Beatrice and Eugenie, the Earl and Countess of Wessex, the Duke and Duchess of Gloucester, Prince and Princess Michael of Kent, and Princess Alexandra were also in the royal convoy.

**LEFT: The Queen and her racing advisor John Warren enjoy a joke as Prince Edward and Princess Michael of Kent look on**

Katherine Jenkins, the Welsh mezzo-soprano, sang the National Anthem from the middle of the course after the Queen alighted from her car. A huge cheer went up as many of the spectators waved Union flags and lined the monarch's route to the stand named in her honour.

The Queen wore a royal blue crêpe wool coat and a white silk dress with blue floral print by Stewart Parvin, teamed with a matching hat by Rachel Trevor-Morgan.

After lunching in the royal box, the balcony of which had been decorated with red, white and blue flowers, it was down to the business of the day, and although the monarch does not bet she likes to take part in a sweepstake for the big race with her guests.

The Derby is the one Classic that has eluded the Queen thus far; despite a great start last year, her horse Carlton House came third. But it won for her at Sandown Park in late May and continues to show great promise.

Her Majesty is thought to have watched TV coverage of the 3:10 race at Haydock Park when her filly Set to Music was beaten into second place.

**RIGHT: The Countess of Wessex looks magnificent in a head-turning hat by milliner Jane Taylor**

**OPPOSITE PAGE: The Queen casts an expert eye over the runners in the paddock before the main race**

Back at Epsom, the royal family were treated to a gala performance by the 8-13 favourite horse, Camelot, which also won this year's 2,000 Guineas race. Trained by Aidan O'Brien and ridden by his 19-year-old son, Joseph, it is the first time a father-and-son duo has won the Derby. Only an hour earlier the Queen met O'Brien junior after presenting the renamed Diamond Jubilee Coronation Cup.

Speaking about the Queen's passion for all things equestrian, Anthony Cane, the racecourse's chairman, said: 'Her knowledge of thoroughbreds and breeding goes way back. She's absolutely amazing.'

The Queen enjoyed her day and as the royal party left the course to drive back to Windsor Castle she must have been happy to see people waiting for her along the roadside for at least 10 miles through Epsom and beyond. This was a special day for everyone.

**BELOW: Princesses Beatrice and Eugenie join their grandfather, the Duke of Edinburgh, in the royal box**

**RIGHT: Joseph O'Brien, who rode winners in two races, receives his Diamond Jubilee Coronation Cup prize from the Queen**

# Jolly Boating Weather?

## By JOE LITTLE

**T**HE BRITISH ARE well known for talking about meteorological matters, and my goodness did we have a lot to talk about on the afternoon the Thames Diamond Jubilee Pageant took place. 'What became of "flaming June?"' people wanted to know. It was cold, grey and later very wet, but nevertheless on Sunday, 3 June an estimated 1.2 million people lined riverbanks, 20-deep in places, balconies and boats to witness the most magnificent flotilla seen on the Thames for more than 250 years.

Everyone was keen to pay tribute to the Queen, even though most got no more than a fleeting glimpse of a tiny 86-year-old woman waving at them in the distance as she sailed past. Yet the monarch was easy to identify from afar, dressed as she was in an ivory-coloured bouclé dress and coat, braided with silk ribbon and with a silk organza frill.

**LEFT: Having passed the Palace of Westminster, the Queen and her family continue their stately progress along the River Thames**

Designed by Angela Kelly, the Queen's senior dresser and personal assistant, the gold and silver embroidered spots and Swarovski crystals (to represent diamonds) would have sparkled in the summer sunshine had there been any. The royal hat had a nautical feel, its swept-up brim ensuring that Her Majesty's face was fully visible. The feathers with which it was decorated were hand-dyed at Buckingham Palace.

The Queen and her Lord High Admiral husband arrived at Chelsea Harbour Pier shortly after 2pm. There to greet them were the Prince of Wales and the Duchess of Cornwall, who chatted with the guard of honour of Chelsea Pensioners as they waited. Two hours earlier Charles and Camilla paid a surprise visit to the Big Jubilee Lunch on Piccadilly, briefly sitting at the 500-seat picnic table among happy but startled diners.

**RIGHT:** The Duke and Duchess of Cambridge and Prince Harry prepare to board the royal barge, *Spirit of Chartwell*

**FAR RIGHT:** The Queen arrives at Chelsea Pier for the start of the spectacular Diamond Jubilee tribute to her

**BELOW:** In all her finery, the royal barge sails under a bridge as she heads downstream towards the Pool of London

'Have you managed to have any lunch yet?' the Prince asked one reveller. Apparently she hadn't. 'We've ruined it!' he exclaimed apologetically.

The Queen's first mode of water-borne transport that afternoon was the tender to HMY *Britannia*, which had been brought down for the occasion from Leith in Edinburgh, where the royal yacht is now moored as a tourist attraction. It was crewed by 'Yotties', former Royal Yachtsmen, much to the monarch's approval.

It was their job to ferry Her Majesty downstream to the *Spirit of Chartwell*, a Thames pleasure cruiser transformed, albeit temporarily, in the preceding months into a stately royal barge complete with gilded carvings, red velvet thrones (never used) and a floral display to rival anything at the Chelsea Flower Show two weeks earlier.

**BELOW: Although the rain held off at the start of the Queen and Prince Philip's voyage, their good luck was soon to run out**

**OPPOSITE PAGE: A lighthearted moment for the two royal duchesses, who formed a close bond long before Kate married William in 2011**

'Spectacular,' was the Queen's verdict.

Already on board the royal barge at Cadogan Pier were the Duke and Duchess of Cambridge: he wore RAF dress uniform, she a pillar-box red Alexander McQueen dress and a matching hat. Prince Harry, dapper in No. 1 ceremonial dress as a captain in the Blues and Royals with an Army Air Corps beret, accompanied them.

Meanwhile, over at Imperial Wharf other members of the royal family were embarking on various vessels. The Duke of York and Princesses Beatrice and Eugenie were on *Havengore* (which carried Churchill's coffin in 1965), as were the Earl and Countess of Wessex, the Duke and Duchess of Gloucester,

and Prince and Princess Michael of Kent. Also on board the vessel were the Mayor of London, Boris Johnson, and the Lord Mayor of London, Alderman David Wootton.

The Princess Royal and Vice-Admiral Sir Tim Laurence boarded Trinity House No. 1 Boat, while the Duke of Kent and his sister Princess Alexandra, sporting a jaunty cap, were on the RNLI *Diamond Jubilee*. The Duchess of Kent, together with the St Andrews' family, the Ogilvys and Lady Frederick Windsor (the former Sophie Winkleman), was on the *Henley*.

Heading the 1,000-boat flotilla was a floating belfry whose eight specially cast bells, all named after a senior member of the royal family, pealed non-stop all the way to Tower Bridge,

some seven miles away. Churches along the route returned the compliment. The bells were later hung at the church of St James Garlickhythe.

Then came the magnificent royal rowbarge, *Gloriana*, the Diamond Jubilee gift presented to the Queen in Greenwich two months earlier.

Having inspected 260 man-powered boats, and vessels from the Commonwealth, the moment had come for Her Majesty's barge to join the procession. The other royal vessels followed, as did the *Elizabethan* with the Middleton family on board.

The flotilla was interspersed with music barges, the soothing Academy of Ancient Music, the rousing Band of Her Majesty's Royal Marines Plymouth, and the fabulous Shree Muktajeevan Pipe Band and Dhol Ensemble among them. Each one received huge cheers from their appreciative audience.

There was fun to be had all the way. As the Queen passed the National Theatre she was pleased to see Joey, the full-sized horse puppet from the play 'War Horse', rearing up in salute, and she called the Duchess of Cornwall over to take a look. Both equestrian-loving women have seen the performance and were enchanted by it.

**LEFT: William, with Kate and Harry behind him, amuses his grandmother with an observation**

**OPPOSITE PAGE: *Gloriana* is rowed by 18 oarsmen and women. The barge now promotes a better use of the Thames**

**LEFT: Princess Michael of Kent captures the amazing scene from the *Havengore***

**BELOW: The Countess of Wessex waves to the participants of the Thames Diamond Jubilee Pageant as they glide past**

**OPPOSITE PAGE: In the background of this photograph of the Duke of York and Earl of Wessex is a huge picture of them with their family on the Buckingham Palace balcony on Silver Jubilee Day in 1977**

It was soon after this that the weather took a turn for the worse, and the heavens opened. The Queen had a canopy under which to shelter, and by this time she had put a shawl around her shoulders. She must have been cold, particularly when the barge went round a bend in the river and sailed headlong into the wind.

A Buckingham Palace spokesman said later that Her Majesty was not bothered because she is used to the climate in Scotland during her summer holiday.

The flotilla continued downstream, the rain getting heavier and the temperature glacial as the bascules of Tower Bridge were raised in salute to the Queen. Once through the bridge the *Spirit of Chartwell* did a 180-degree turn and went alongside HMS *President*; it was from here that Her Majesty watched the hundreds of vessels pass by, horns tooting and klaxons sounding in acknowledgement of the distinctive regal wave.

Much to my surprise, the *Havengore* moored alongside the boat from which I was viewing proceedings, her passengers royal or otherwise looking chilled to the bone.

'You've got to be cold,' I said to the Countess of Wessex. 'Freezing!' was her emphatic reply.

**RIGHT: Princesses Beatrice and Eugenie fly the flag from the deck of the *Havengore***

**BELOW: *Gloriana*, at the head of the Thames Diamond Jubilee Pageant, reaches HMS *Belfast***

For the next hour and a half vessels of all shapes and sizes sailed by: Dunkirk's 'Little Ships', historic and service vessels, working boats, leisure boats, narrow boats and passengers boats. An 'Avenue of Sail', vessels from around the world that were too large to travel with the rest of the flotilla, was formed on both banks above and below Tower Bridge, enhancing the historic backdrop.

Relief from the unseasonable chill eventually came in the form of the London Philharmonic Orchestra. As their barge approached they played the 'Sailor's Hornpipe', which, as many people will know, gets faster and faster as it goes on. The tradition is to bob up and down in time to the music, and sure enough the royal parties on either side of the river did just that, much to their amusement when the tune ended.

The orchestra brought the pageant to a close with the National Anthem, after which fireworks were let off on Tower Bridge. The flypast of Royal Navy helicopters in a diamond formation intended as part of the finale was cancelled because of the atrocious weather.

Pageant Master Adrian Evans and his team were rightly praised – and later rewarded – for putting together an event (over several years) that we will never forget, such was their attention to detail, but equally memorable is the fact that the Queen and Prince Philip – seven days away from his 91st birthday – were on their feet in challenging conditions for four hours, not wanting to miss a thing.

What a remarkable couple they proved to be that day.

**OPPOSITE PAGE: The Queen chats with her daughter-in-law as they sail past the National Theatre and South Bank complex**

**BELOW: The Princess Royal, Chief Commandant for Women in the Royal Navy, and Vice-Admiral Tim Laurence acknowledge the cheers of the crowd**

# The Show Must Go On

## By INGRID SEWARD

**Q**UEEN VICTORIA MIGHT not have been amused at her memorial being used for a concert, but her great-great-granddaughter clearly didn't mind. Having had supper on a card table in front of the television, the Queen knew exactly what was going on and when her moment came she was clearly ready to rock.

Dressed in another Angela Kelly creation – this time a gold lamé cocktail dress with antique lace detail glittering with her now trademark Swarovski crystals – the Queen was escorted by the Prince of Wales and Duchess of Cornwall to her place in the royal box at exactly 9pm for the remainder of the concert. Wrapped up against the evening chill in an admiral's boat cloak, possibly the one in which Cecil Beaton photographed her in 1968, she was without the Duke of Edinburgh for the first time during the Diamond Jubilee weekend.

Earlier in the day Prince Philip was taken by ambulance from Windsor Castle to King Edward VII Hospital for Officers in central London suffering from a bladder infection serious enough to warrant hospitalisation.

If the Queen was daunted by his absence she did not show it and the crowd roared their appreciation as she sat down between Prince Charles and her son-in-law (and former equerry) Tim Laurence.

**LEFT: The Prince of Wales gives a warm, witty and emotional speech in praise of his mother as the Diamond Jubilee concert ends**

Robbie Williams, who had opened the concert with his rendition of *Let Me Entertain You*, sang something gentler for the Queen: a Sinatra-like version of *Mack the Knife*. The evening was so expertly choreographed it appeared like one continuous snake of six decades of musical hits performed by unusually well dressed superstars. Cheryl Cole wore a fishtail dress of such vast proportions that she had to be helped up the steps after her duet with Gary Barlow. Jessie J (who sang with rapper Will.i.am) wore the winning outfit for me, a figure-hugging sparkly long dress embroidered with Union Jacks.

While Sir Cliff Richard sang a medley of songs from each decade of the Queen's reign, home movies of her were projected on to giant screens and later 64-year-old Grace Jones put us to shame as she sang *Slave to the Rhythm*, all the while spinning a hula-hoop around her waist. Of course Sir Tom Jones belted out *Delilah*, which raised a spark from Prince Harry, who sang along in the royal box while the others waved Union flags.

Sir Elton John performed *Your Song* and *Crocodile Rock*, while Motown legend Stevie Wonder sang *Isn't She Lovely* and *Happy Birthday*, and accompanied Annie Lennox on the harmonica for *There Must Be an Angel*. On a night like this Dame Shirley Bassey could only ever sing one song: *Diamonds are Forever*.

**LEFT:** The Queen acknowledges the crowd as she takes her seat in the royal box for the second half of the concert in her honour

**BELOW:** *Let Me Entertain You*, Robbie Williams sings, getting the show off to a lively start

When the group Madness took to the roof of the most famous address in the world to sing *Our House*, they changed the lyrics to 'Our house, in the middle of one's street', while an animated projection of a council block appeared on the front of Buckingham Palace.

The displays and pyrotechnics throughout the concert were amazing, with more than 600 crew employed backstage. This might sound a lot, but for a concert of this magnitude with so many huge stars it is nothing. Most performers have their own backing group, their own technicians and their own people with them. The logistics for this concert were unprecedented since not only did they accommodate all the musicians but also at one point had over 100 singers on stage when the Commonwealth group performed the Jubilee song *Sing*, written by Lord Lloyd Webber and Gary Barlow.

The Queen is well known for her middle-of-the-road musical taste and her fondness for the hits from musicals of the Forties and Fifties, but on this occasion she enjoyed everything. It was said she fell in love with Prince Philip to the sounds of *People Will Say We're in Love* from 'Oklahoma', but she also enjoys Sir Elton John's music. He has performed for her on several occasions; significantly at Prince Andrew's 21st birthday party at Windsor Castle, when Elton was far more outrageous than he is now.

**OPPOSITE PAGE: Sir Elton John has the crowd singing along lustily to the chorus of one of his greatest hits, *Crocodile Rock***

**Australian chanteuse Kylie Minogue takes to the stage on the Queen Victoria Memorial in a pearly queen-style outfit**

**The much-loved Annie Lennox sings *There Must Be An Angel* dressed in the most appropriate way: as an angel**

**BELOW: Lady Sarah Chatto, the Duke and Duchess of Cambridge and Zara Phillips are definitely having a good time**

A poignant moment for the Queen must have been when soprano Renée Fleming and tenor Alfie Boe were floodlit standing at the window of the Chinese Dining Room in Buckingham Palace (where the Queen recorded her address on the eve of Diana's funeral) singing *There's a Place for Us* from 'West Side Story'.

Although *Majesty* managing editor Joe Little and I had missed the picnic that afternoon in the Buckingham Palace garden, attended by 10,000 ballot winners, we were very fortunate to have prime-position seats in the temporary amphitheatre constructed by the BBC. Up to half a million people in The Mall, St James's Park and Hyde Park watched on enormous screens. The picnic was especially designed so that people would have a chance to wander around the gardens of Buckingham Palace and enjoy a hamper of delicious goodies created by superchef Heston Blumenthal and royal chef Mark Flanagan.

The Countess of Wessex and her York nieces, Princesses Beatrice and Eugenie, strolled around the garden, chatting to as many people as possible before the concert began.

**OPPOSITE PAGE: The jaw-dropping view from the roof of Buckingham Palace, with spectators as far as the eye could see**

**BELOW: William and Harry enter into the spirit of the occasion, staged, according to one comedian, in their grandmother's 'front garden'**

'Diamonds are Forever,' Dame Shirley Bassey insists; the star-struck audience had no reason to disagree

OPPOSITE PAGE: The Prince of Wales gallantly kisses 'Mummy' on the hand after his heartfelt tribute to her

The occupants of the royal box were an eclectic mix of former prime ministers, past and present members of the Royal Household including Lord Fellowes and his wife Jane (sister of the late Diana, Princess of Wales), the Archbishop of Canterbury and most of the royal family, with a rare public appearance by the Duchess of Kent, a real music lover.

The Duchess of Cambridge, sitting between Princess Beatrice and Prince William, wore a dress from the high-street store Whistles and an Alexander McQueen jacket while William and Harry, Mike Tindall, Peter Phillips and David Linley were tieless but wore jackets as a concession to the Queen's presence.

Sir Paul McCartney brought the show to a close with his rendition of classic Beatles hits, including *Ob-La-Di Ob-La-Da*, which was projected on to the front of the palace as all the acts came on to the stage to wait for the by now cloak-less Queen and the Prince of Wales.

Charles gave a warm and witty speech in praise of his mother, which, just as he had done 10 years earlier, he began with the words 'Your Majesty – Mummy'. He touchingly made reference to his father in hospital and suggested that if the crowd cheered loud enough the Duke might hear them.

A spectacular fireworks display lights up the sky over a red, white and blue Buckingham Palace

OPPOSITE PAGE:
The Queen is amused by comedian Peter Kay, as were her family during his performance

There were repeated chants of 'Philip! Philip! Philip!' which appeared to move the Queen, before Prince Charles ended his remarks by addressing his mother: 'As a nation this is our opportunity to thank you and my father for always being there for us. For inspiring us with your selfless duty and service and for making us proud to be British.'

To roars from the crowd the Prince led the audience in giving three cheers for the Queen before he kissed her hand. The National Anthem played and the Queen then lit the National Beacon by placing a 'Jubilee Crystal' into a specially designed pod, triggering the automatic ignition of the 28ft-high beacon in The Mall, sending a rush of flame into the sky.

It was the last in a chain of 4,200 beacons that formed a symbolic ring of light around the globe. A phenomenal fireworks finale then burst into life.

As we made our way home in an affable throng of many thousands, I am sure we all felt proud to be British. Meanwhile, the Queen was meeting and thanking the entertainers, but she left it to the younger members of the family to host what could have been the party of all parties in the Marble Hall and Bow Room at Buckingham Palace.

It ended at 1am but, had it not been for the service of thanksgiving at St Paul's later that morning, with seasoned partygoers such as Prince Harry, Zara Phillips and her husband Mike Tindall present I suspect it might have gone on for much longer.

# The Nation Gives Thanks

## By JOE LITTLE

The Queen, with the Prince of Wales and the Duchess of Cornwall, attends the national service of thanksgiving in St Paul's Cathedral

**W**HEN THE QUEEN stepped on to the balcony at Buckingham Palace on 5 June for a Royal Air Force flypast the noise of the crowd must have been quite overwhelming. Before her an estimated one million people had congregated around the Queen Victoria Memorial and right down The Mall, almost all waving flags and cheering wildly as they caught sight of the much-loved monarch whose milestone moment they were celebrating.

For the Golden Jubilee in 2002 there had been some 20 members of the royal family on the balcony; this time their number had been pared down to just six. Underlining the endurance of the British monarchy, Queen Elizabeth II was flanked by her heir, the Prince of Wales, and his eventual successor, the Duke of Cambridge. The Duchesses of Cornwall and Cambridge, and Prince Harry, were present, but of course the Duke of Edinburgh should have been there too, supporting his wife in the exemplary way that he has done throughout her reign.

Prince Philip's absence cast a long shadow over the final two days of festivities, it has to be said. The Queen, dutiful as ever, put on a brave face but occasionally the mask slipped and, unusually for her, she appeared frail and forlorn. Her children and adult grandchildren seemed equally distracted at times.

A moment for quiet and solitary reflection for the Queen during the service to mark her 60-year reign

**LEFT:** Her Majesty and her family sit under the dome of the cathedral, around them the 2,000-strong congregation

'She's bearing up but missing him, obviously,' the Earl of Wessex said after visiting the Duke of Edinburgh in hospital that afternoon.

The day of ceremonial began at St Paul's Cathedral, where a congregation of more than 2,000 people – friends, past and present staff, government, politicians and representatives of the many organisations with which the Queen is linked (and me) – assembled inside Wren's masterpiece for a national service of thanksgiving. Providing a riot of colour on an otherwise dull day were the Queen's Body Guard of the Yeomen of the Guard, Her Majesty's Body Guard of the Honourable Corps of Gentlemen at Arms, and the Kings of Arms, Heralds and Pursuivants.

It was all very different in Queen Victoria's day, as has been well documented, and when a service was held to mark her Diamond Jubilee on 22 June 1897 it took place on the steps of the cathedral. The infirm matriarch – eight years younger than her sprightly great-great-granddaughter – remained seated in her open carriage.

In 1897 the royal family travelled to and from the cathedral in a lengthy and most impressive procession of horse-drawn carriages and mounted troops from all over the British Empire, but in 2012 the horsepower was of a different kind: minibuses, coaches and cars. I understand it was the Queen who decided not to use the Gold State Coach on this occasion.

When a huge roar from the enthusiastic crowd outside could be heard within the cathedral we realised that Her Majesty, accompanied by Diana, Lady Farnham, one of her team of ladies-in-waiting, had arrived in her State Bentley. The cheers got louder and louder, completely drowning the heckling of a handful of republican protestors.

The Queen, wearing an outfit by Angela Kelly, leaves the cathedral after the service

OPPOSITE PAGE: The Duke and Duchess of Cambridge and Prince Harry listen to the Archbishop of Canterbury's address

The Queen was in yet another stunning Angela Kelly creation: a mint green dress and coat of fine silk tulle embellished with silver thread and tiny star-shaped flowers, and a chiffon drape with Swarovski crystals on the shoulders. The crown of the hat was in the same material as the coat.

A fanfare having sounded, the monarch walked down the aisle alone behind the Lord Mayor of the City of London, who was carrying the pearl sword brought out for the grandest of occasions, but she sat beside her family under the dome of the cathedral rather than in front of them as she would have done had her husband been present. It was a small gesture but no doubt it brought her some comfort.

Of all the events to mark the Queen's Diamond Jubilee, this was probably the most important to Her Majesty, such is the strength of her Christian belief. She was nine years old when she celebrated the Silver Jubilee of her grandfather King George V in the same setting in 1935, and her own Silver Jubilee and Golden Jubilee services were held at St Paul's Cathedral in 1977 and 2002 respectively. Consequently, she was very familiar with the words and music of the three hymns: *All People That On Earth Do Dwell*, *O Praise Ye The Lord*, and *Guide Me, O Thou Great Redeemer*.

'We come to this cathedral church today to give thanks to almighty God for the prosperous reign of the Queen and to rejoice together in this year of Her Majesty's Jubilee as we celebrate 60 years of her sovereignty and service,' said the Very Reverend David Ison, the recently installed Dean of St Paul's, as he began the Bidding.

**BELOW: Princess Alexandra, a first cousin of the Queen, is among the many members of the royal family present that morning**

**BELOW LEFT: Eugenie wears a purple dress by designer Suzannah, while sister Beatrice opts for a cornflower blue outfit by Kinder Aggugini**

**OPPOSITE PAGE: The Queen and the Dean of St Paul's view an inscription to mark Queen Victoria's Diamond Jubilee service in June 1897**

'As we come together as loyal subjects from all parts of the realms and commonwealth of nations, we give thanks for the blessings bestowed by God on our Sovereign Lady Queen Elizabeth, and we celebrate the identity and variety which our nations under her have enjoyed,' the Dean said.

The Prime Minister, David Cameron, read the lesson from *Romans 12*: 'Let love be genuine; hate what is evil, hold fast to what is good; love one another with mutual affection; outdo one another in showing affection.'

The monarch listened intently as Dr Rowan Williams, the Archbishop of Canterbury, spoke of her overwhelming dedication to duty.

'I don't think it's at all fanciful to say that, in all her public engagements, our Queen has shown a quality of joy in the happiness of others,' he said. 'She has made her "public" happy and all the signs are that she is herself happy, fulfilled and at home in these encounters.

**CLOCKWISE FROM LEFT: Lord Frederick Windsor and his wife Sophie attend the reception**

**The Princess Royal and her daughter Zara Phillips in conversation with the Prime Minister, David Cameron, at Guildhall**

**Lady Helen Taylor and Autumn Phillips pose for a photograph**

**OPPOSITE PAGE: The Countess of Wessex with her eight-year-old daughter, Lady Louise Mountbatten-Windsor**

**The Duchess of Cambridge looks stunning in a nude lace dress by Alexander McQueen and a matching Jane Taylor hat**

**Accompanied by a Sovereign's Escort, the Queen is driven along Whitehall in the 1902 State Landau**

**OPPOSITE PAGE: In Prince Philip's absence, the Duchess of Cornwall sits alongside Her Majesty**

'To declare a lifelong dedication is to take a huge risk, to embark on a costly venture. But it is also to respond to the promise of a vision that brings joy.

'The same of course can be said about Prince Philip,' the Archbishop continued, in a last-minute addition to his sermon. 'Our prayers and thoughts are with him this morning.'

When the hour-long service was over, the Queen and her family left to the strains of *Orb and Sceptre*, written by William Walton for her coronation in 1953, and *Pomp and Circumstance March No. 4*, by Edward Elgar. Uplifting music is good for even the most troubled of souls.

Her Majesty then attended a reception at Mansion House hosted by the Lord Mayor of the City of London, the Court of Alderman and the Court of Common Council for 250 guests, while the rest of the St Paul's congregation, including the royal family, went to a second Corporation of London reception at Guildhall.

The Queen later drove to Westminster Hall for the Diamond Jubilee luncheon, given in her honour by City livery companies. She was accompanied by the Prince of Wales and the Duchess of Cornwall, the Duke and Duchess of Cambridge and Prince Harry.

The Master Mercer, Thomas Sheldon, gave a short speech, after which the Speaker of the House of Commons said Grace.

Representatives from livery companies were present at the luncheon, but the vast majority of the 700-strong guest list comprised people from all over the country whose trade, craft or profession was represented by the different liveries taking part in the event, together with the charities, schools and other organisations they support.

The National Children's Orchestra of Great Britain performed during the luncheon.

Afterwards the royal party left for Buckingham Palace in a carriage procession, scaled down from three carriages to two because of the Duke of Edinburgh's absence. Under a dark grey sky, the Queen, travelling now with the Prince of Wales and the Duchess of Cornwall, used the 1902 State Landau, while William, Kate and Harry followed in a second landau.

The royal party were accompanied by a Sovereign's Escort. Their route, lined by personnel from all three Services, took them up Whitehall to Trafalgar Square, through Admiralty Arch and along The Mall, which the police had declared 'full' hours before the procession.

When the Queen alighted from her carriage at the Grand Entrance she was presented with a posy of flowers by Philippa Jackson, a coachman from the Royal Mews, who should have been on the third carriage. Her Majesty seemed touched by the gesture.

The 45 minutes until the flypast gave the police time to bring the good-natured crowd of well-wishers towards the palace in a much-practised 'rolling roadblock'. It was the incredible sight of one-million-plus people standing there in heavy rain that took the Queen's breath away; the Duchess of Cambridge had the same experience on her wedding day a year earlier.

The Queen waves to the huge crowd that had gathered to see her, many of whom had been there since early morning

OPPOSITE PAGE: The Red Arrows trail red, white and blue vapour as they fly over Buckingham Palace

Her Majesty was visibly moved by the reaction from the crowd. It was one of the most joyous moments in her reign – but it was also tinged with sadness; her deepest regret was that Prince Philip was unable to share it with her. We discovered later that he had watched the events on television.

'It's a pity he couldn't be here with me today,' the Queen said to Prince Charles, according to professional lip-readers also watching on television. 'An incredible day and afternoon…' she is said to have added. 'It's been wonderful.'

The monarch and her family watched the flypast of the Battle of Britain Memorial Flight followed by an impressive display by the Red Arrows complete with patriotic red, white and blue smoke trails. For only the second time in the present reign there followed a *feu de joie* (fire of joy) from the palace forecourt – a celebratory cascade of rifle fire given as a salute by the Queen's Guard, interspersed with the National Anthem played by the Band of the Irish Guards.

Even after four hectic days of activities the 86-year-old Queen

could not put her feet up. That evening she gave a reception at Buckingham Palace for governor-generals visiting the United Kingdom, and the following morning received the prime ministers of Canada and New Zealand before a luncheon for Commonwealth heads of government at Marlborough House, which was hosted by the Right Honourable Kamalesh Sharma, the Commonwealth Secretary-General.

Buckingham Palace subsequently revealed that the Queen received an exceptional number of letters and messages of goodwill following the Diamond Jubilee weekend, taking the total to over 130,000 letters and messages at that stage. Some 45 sacks of mail were delivered in just three days.

This includes over 60,000 'Jubilee' letters and more than 71,000 electronic messages of congratulations through the official Diamond Jubilee website.

**BELOW: A pared-down royal family of just six key players appear on the palace balcony for the finale of the Queen's Diamond Jubilee Weekend**

**The Queen shortly after arriving in Northern Ireland for a two-day Diamond Jubilee visit**

# Peace Process

## By RICHARD PALMER

QUEEN ELIZABETH II'S Diamond Jubilee visit to Northern Ireland will go down in the annals as a seismic event in Anglo-Irish relations and a pivotal moment in the troubled province's history.

The Queen was in Northern Ireland for the 20th time in her 60-year reign, ostensibly to mark her jubilee, but enhanced her reputation as the leading stateswoman of her age by taking part in a series of engagements that turned convention on its head and set the seal on a 14-year peace process.

In a courageous personal act of reconciliation, she met and shook hands for the first time with Sinn Féin's Northern Ireland Deputy First Minister Martin McGuinness, a former IRA commander suspected of approving the assassination in 1979 of Earl Mountbatten of Burma, her second cousin once removed, favoured counsellor and Prince Philip's uncle and surrogate father.

It was a meeting unthinkable only a few years ago even after the IRA ended a 30-year armed conflict and signed up to the 1998 Anglo-Irish Agreement. But it underscored the personal commitment the Queen gave to the peace process last year when she visited the Irish Republic for the first time and went much further than many expected in acknowledging mistakes on all sides and sharing her family's grief with the relatives of the 3,600 military, police and civilian dead of the Troubles.

When the Queen visited Northern Ireland for her Silver Jubilee in 1977 there was so much political and sectarian violence she was warned not to come amid fears a visit would enflame the mobs. She had to stay on *Britannia* and was flown to her engagements by helicopter.

This time cheering crowds greeted her wherever she went in areas dominated by the Union flag-waving Protestant majority in the six counties separated by partition in 1921 when the rest of Ireland gained independence from Britain.

But, more significantly, the Queen was also given a warm welcome by many in the formerly downtrodden republican and nationalist minority after setting foot in a Roman Catholic church in Northern Ireland for the first time.

Ominously, the two-day visit got off to an inauspicious start when low cloud, high winds and heavy rain meant the royal plane could not land at Enniskillen in Co. Fermanagh. They had to fly to RAF Aldergrove near Belfast and take a helicopter from there, arriving almost an hour late.

In the town centre, several hundred people had waited for hours in the cold, wind and rain to see the Queen and they screamed their approval when she and the Duke of Edinburgh finally arrived to attend an ecumenical thanksgiving service in the Anglican St Macartin's Cathedral.

Next door in the deanery, the Queen met victims of one of the IRA's worst atrocities, 25 years after 11 people died and 63 were wounded in a Poppy Day bomb attack on families commemorating the dead of two world wars at a service of remembrance in the town.

'She was very sympathetic to us. She was very gracious. I am absolutely honoured that she came to Enniskillen,' said Margaret Veitch, whose parents William and Nessie Mullan died in the bombing.

As bells pealed and thousands of people cheered, the Queen and Prince Philip broke new ground, walking 20 yards across the road into St Michael's Parish Church, their first visit to a Roman Catholic church in the province, to meet representatives from schools, sports clubs and organisations from various religious backgrounds.

**LEFT:** The Queen wears a Wedgwood blue crêpe wool coat with lace decoration and matching hat

**BELOW:** Schoolchildren wave Union flags as they wait for the delayed monarch in Enniskillen

**RIGHT:** Among Her Majesty's first engagements was a visit to South West Acute Hospital

Historic handshake: Her Majesty smiles broadly as she bids farewell to Martin McGuinness

OPPOSITE PAGE: The Queen walks past schoolchildren after touring the *Titanic* Centre in Belfast

Frank O'Reilly, 63, a driving instructor and former choirboy who has sung in the church for 50 years, joined others in performing traditional hymns for the royal couple.

'Given the present climate this has been a huge step forward for the Catholic and Nationalist communities,' he said.

The Queen, who was wearing a Wedgwood blue outfit and hat by Angela Kelly and a shamrock diamond brooch, then went on an impromptu walkabout outside to meet some of the hundreds of residents who had been patiently waiting to catch a glimpse of her.

Later, she opened the new South West Acute Hospital in Enniskillen, where the 86-year-old monarch met Conall Corrigan, eight, who asked her where her crown was. 'I don't always bring it with me,' she replied.

After a night spent at Hillsborough Castle, her official residence in the province, the Queen met Mr McGuinness the next morning at an event celebrating arts and culture across the entire island at Belfast's new £18 million Lyric Theatre, a symbol of the new Northern Ireland. Amid fears of protests and potential attacks by dissidents, police sealed off the streets around the venue and told residents to stay in their homes.

It must have been difficult for the Queen and the Duke of Edinburgh, who were left bereft after Lord Mountbatten and members of his family were blown up by an IRA bomb attack on his fishing boat in County Sligo in August 1979.

Sixty-two-year-old Mr McGuinness has insisted he had left the IRA by 1974, but British and Irish officials and most serious historians of the conflict maintain that he was a senior figure on the IRA Army Council between 1971 and 2005 and therefore must have had advance knowledge of the Mountbatten murders.

**The Queen and Prince Philip are driven around the Stormont estate in an open-top vehicle**

But after their meeting at the Co-operation Ireland event in the Lyric Theatre both sides said it had been a relaxed and cordial encounter. 'The Queen has always been very open to this, particularly after the success of her visit to Ireland last year,' a royal source confirmed. 'She was very relaxed and animated.'

Mr McGuinness, who once served a prison sentence for membership of the IRA after being caught with a car containing 250lbs of explosives and nearly 5,000 rounds of ammunition, told the Queen that families on both sides had suffered during those years of conflict. The monarch, wearing an Angela Kelly apple-green outfit in a nod to the Irish, agreed, according to a Sinn Féin source, who said they discussed the need to build on the peace process.

'I represent people that have been terribly hurt by British state violence over the course of many years,' Mr McGuinness said. 'But I am also big enough to understand that Queen Elizabeth has also lost a loved one, and of course there are families in Britain, mothers, fathers, sisters and brothers, children of people who were sent here as British soldiers who lost their lives also.'

He greeted the Queen in Gaelic, saying: '*Maidin mhaith* – Good morning – and *Céad mile fáilte* – A hundred thousand welcomes,' as they shook hands in private in a side room with Irish President Michael D. Higgins and a small group of other dignitaries watching.

When they shook hands again, this time in public before the monarch left, Mr McGuinness said: '*Slán agus beannacht*', translating the traditional blessing as 'Goodbye and God speed', although others said it meant 'Health and happiness'. Philip too shook his hand.

Their duty done, the royal couple went off to see Belfast's £97 million *Titanic* visitor attraction, which tells the story of the famous liner's construction in the city and its sinking in April 1912 on its maiden voyage from Southampton to New York with the loss of more than 1,500 lives.

After a lunch featuring Guinness and treacle bread, salmon, chicken and lemon curd tart, they finished their two-day visit in triumph, touring the grounds of the Stormont estate in east Belfast in an open-top car to the cheers of 25,000 people who had turned up for a jubilee party.

'This is a moment in Northern Ireland's history that will shine in our collective memory,' the Northern Ireland Secretary Owen Paterson said. 'It's been a very special visit, in a very special Diamond Jubilee year. The warmth and respect for the Queen demonstrated by the people of Northern Ireland has been overwhelming.'

**FROM FAR LEFT: Thousands of people gather in front of Parliament Buildings to see the Queen and the Duke of Edinburgh**

**Their two-day visit at an end, the royal couple are given a rousing send-off from Stormont**

**Her Majesty's striking apple-green outfit has gold detailing on the collar and hat, plus a gold feather for good measure**

# June

A S THE DIAMOND JUBILEE WEEKEND drew to a close, the Queen made a televised broadcast to the nation and the Commonwealth. The special message of thanks was recorded in the Presence Room at Buckingham Palace prior to the concert on 4 June:

'The events that I have attended to mark my Diamond Jubilee have been a humbling experience. It has touched me deeply to see so many thousands of families, neighbours and friends celebrating together in such a happy atmosphere.

'But Prince Philip and I want to take this opportunity to offer our special thanks and appreciation to all those who have had a hand in organising these Jubilee celebrations. It has been a massive challenge, and I am sure that everyone who has enjoyed these festive occasions realises how much work has been involved.

'I hope that memories of all this year's happy events will brighten our lives for many years to come. I will continue to treasure and draw inspiration from the countless kindnesses shown to me in this country and throughout the Commonwealth.

'Thank you all.'

**RIGHT:** The Duchess of Cambridge laughs when her husband throws a children's foam javelin in Vernon Park, Nottingham

**OPPOSITE PAGE:** 'There's nothing I can do,' the Queen gestures as her grandson is mobbed by the excited sports event crowd

The Queen visited the East Midlands on 13 and 14 June, and was accompanied on the first day, in Nottingham, by the Duke and Duchess of Cambridge. The Duke of Edinburgh should also have been present, but he was recuperating from the bladder infection that laid him low a week earlier.

William and Kate were at Nottingham railway station to meet his grandmother, and from there they proceeded to the Market Square, where they went on a short walkabout. Having entered Nottingham Council House, they made a balcony appearance before attending a reception in the ballroom.

The royal party then travelled to Vernon Park to mark a Fields in Trust project for the Diamond Jubilee. William, as Patron of the Queen Elizabeth Fields Challenge – one of the projects supported by the Royal Foundation of the Duke and Duchess of Cambridge and Prince Harry – made a short speech.

'The occasion presents the perfect opportunity for me, through my patronage of the Queen Elizabeth II Fields, to pay tribute to the Queen on her Diamond Jubilee,' he said.

'On behalf of Fields in Trust, thank you so much Your Majesty and the Duke of Edinburgh for everything you have done throughout your reign to protect these vital outdoor places for the nation. How grateful we are for the extraordinary love and devotion you have shown to the people of this country and the Commonwealth.'

**FROM TOP: The Queen with Commonwealth leaders after a luncheon at Marlborough House on 6 June**

**The Earl and Countess of Wessex visit the Upper Rock during a three-day Diamond Jubilee trip to Gibraltar**

**OPPOSITE PAGE: Her Majesty unveils the Canadian Diamond Jubilee portrait at Buckingham Palace**

His speech brought an ecstatic response from the crowd in Vernon Park.

The Queen's Diamond Jubilee tour then continued to Burghley House, near Stamford in Lincolnshire, while the Cambridges stayed to talk to people involved in the Queen Elizabeth Fields Challenge.

Some 10,000 people from voluntary groups in Lincolnshire, Cambridgeshire, Rutland and Northamptonshire joined the monarch for a picnic. Her Majesty planted a tree near one Queen Victoria planted for her own Diamond Jubilee in 1897.

**OPPOSITE PAGE: The Queen gives a garden party at Sandringham House in Norfolk on 12 June to mark her 60-year reign**

**BELOW: The Duchess of Cornwall visits a celebration of the Queen's Diamond Jubilee in flowers at St Mary's Church in Barnes, southwest London**

1

The Queen concluded her working day in Corby, Northamptonshire. She visited the East Midlands International Pool, where she watched diving and snorkelling displays, and The Cube, which houses council offices, a library and a theatre.

Next morning, the Queen toured the packed Market Square at Hitchin in Hertfordshire to meet shopkeepers and watch a presentation by local schoolchildren.

The monarch then went on to Lister Hospital in Stevenage, where she opened the Diamond Jubilee Maternity Unit, and was shown some of the new arrivals and talked to their parents.

The Queen later visited Hatfield House, the historic home of the 7th Marquess of Salisbury, who helped mastermind the Thames Diamond Jubilee Pageant.

Her Majesty planted a 'Diamond Jubilee tree' in the park before attending a drinks reception and lunch at Hatfield House. It was in an earlier royal palace at Hatfield that the future Queen Elizabeth I spent her childhood.

**OPPOSITE PAGE:** The Queen and Prince Philip travel to Henley Business School on *Alaska* for a three-counties garden party

**BELOW:** Her Majesty meets entrants in the Diamond Jubilee 'Cook for the Queen' competition at Buckingham Palace

# Holyrood Week

By JOE LITTLE

THE QUEEN AND the Duke of Edinburgh annually undertake a variety of engagements in Scotland to celebrate Scottish culture, history and achievement – and this year, Her Majesty's Diamond Jubilee too. 'Holyrood Week', as the occasion is known, invariably begins with the Ceremony of the Keys in the forecourt of Edinburgh's Palace of Holyroodhouse, during which the Lord Provost officially receives the Queen. Such was the case on 2 July when Her Majesty was presented with the keys of the city and welcomed to her 'ancient and hereditary kingdom of Scotland'. In keeping with tradition the monarch returned the keys to the city's elected officials for safekeeping.

The Queen and the Duke of Edinburgh then visited the Scottish National Portrait Gallery, where a large crowd had gathered to welcome them. The New Town building, which reopened in December 2011 following a £17.6m restoration project, houses works by some of the most important artists in history as well as portraits of great Scots. It also contains the world's most comprehensive collection of Scottish art.

In the evening Prince Philip attended Duke of Edinburgh Gold Award presentations at the palace.

Presentations of a different kind were made the following morning when the Queen held an investiture ceremony in the Great Gallery at the Palace of Holyroodhouse to enable Scottish residents whose achievements have been recognised in the twice-yearly honours' list to collect their awards from Her Majesty in their home country.

Television presenter Lorraine Kelly, who was made an Officer of the Most Excellent Order of the British Empire in recognition of her charity work, was among the recipients and later admitted to being tearful as she stepped forward to receive her insignia from the Queen.

More than 70 people from fields including medicine, the arts, business and the voluntary sector collected honours during the hour-long ceremony.

That afternoon the Queen and the Duke of Edinburgh entertained some 8,000 guests from all walks of Scottish life at a garden party in the grounds of the palace, which stands at the foot of Edinburgh's Royal Mile.

**LEFT: The monarch encounters Queen Anne, when Princess of Denmark, as she tours the Scottish National Portrait Gallery in Edinburgh**

The guests enjoyed tea in the gardens accompanied by music from regimental bands and the Royal Scottish Pipers' Society. It was King George V and Queen Mary who held the first garden party at Holyroodhouse and the tradition has been maintained ever since.

The Royal Company of Archers were on duty at the garden party. Since its appointment as the Sovereign's Body Guard in Scotland in 1822 for the visit of King George IV to Edinburgh, the Royal Company of Archers has served as bodyguard to each successive monarch. In this role today it is available for duty anywhere in Scotland at the request of the monarch on any state and ceremonial occasion that may be taking place.

Indeed, the Royal Company of Archers were on duty in Glasgow Cathedral the following morning at an ecumenical service of thanksgiving led by the Reverend Dr Laurence Whitley to mark the Queen's Diamond Jubilee.

Leading religious figures, including Cardinal Keith O'Brien, head of the Roman Catholic Church in Scotland, the Most Reverend Mario Conti, Archbishop of Glasgow, and the Right Reverend Albert Bogle, Moderator of the General Assembly, were among the 1,300-strong congregation.

The Lady Saltoun, who is a member of the extended royal family through her marriage to the late Captain Alexander Ramsay of Mar, was present, along with military figures and politicians including Scotland's First Minister, Alex Salmond. He read the first lesson.

The Fanfare Trumpeters of the Band of Her Majesty's Royal Marines Scotland sounded a fanfare as the Queen and Prince Philip entered the cathedral and formed part of a royal procession that included banner bearers and heralds who progressed up the central aisle to the quire.

In his sermon, the Right Reverend Bogle paid tribute to the Queen. 'During this past 60 years Her Majesty has brought the continuity and insight of a wise and gifted monarch, acting as a counsellor and confidante to many a prime minister and world leader,' he said.

Concluding with a jubilee prayer, he added: 'We give you thanks and praise that you have blessed this nation, the realms and territories with Elizabeth, our beloved and glorious Queen.'

Pupils from secondary schools around Glasgow read prayers of thanksgiving. Church leaders, including the Most Reverend David Chillingworth, Primus of the Scottish Episcopal Church, also said prayers.

**LEFT: The Queen receives Scotland's First Minister Alex Salmond in audience**

**OPPOSITE PAGE: Her Majesty gives an afternoon party in the Palace of Holyroodhouse gardens**

The Queen and the Duke of Edinburgh meet members of the public in George Square in Glasgow

OPPOSITE PAGE: Her Majesty leaves Glasgow Cathedral after the Scottish service of thanksgiving

After the service, the Queen and the Duke drove to Glasgow's George Square, where they met community leaders in a marquee decorated with red, white and blue bunting.

She and Prince Philip later visited St Margaret's Hospice in Clydebank, West Dunbartonshire, to meet patients and staff. They were greeted by hundreds of flag-waving residents.

Hugh McElroy, the manager of the hospice's charity shop, was a young army cadet when he last saw the Queen in the early 1960s. 'She has changed colossally since then,' he said. 'But she remains as elegant and social as ever.'

The royal visitors attended a lunch in the grounds of Our Holy Redeemer Primary School, Clydebank. Afterwards, they travelled to Cathcart Square in Greenock, where the Queen opened Inverclyde Council's £2 million offices in Greenock Municipal Buildings.

As with all the Diamond Jubilee visits, thousands of people cheered and waved to the royal couple, and in return were rewarded with a walkabout.

The Duke of Cambridge was installed as a Knight of the Thistle at St Giles' Cathedral in Edinburgh on 5 July at a service attended by the Queen, the Duke of Edinburgh, the Princess Royal, the Duchess of Cambridge and hundreds of invited guests.

Thousands of people crowded on to the Royal Mile to catch a glimpse of William and Kate – known as the Earl and Countess of Strathearn while in Scotland – as they travelled to the cathedral in a motorcar procession.

The Order of the Thistle is the highest honour in Scotland and is second only in precedence in the United Kingdom to the Order of the Garter. It honours men and women who have held public office or contributed in a significant way to national life.

The royal family arrived at the west door of the cathedral shortly before 11am to a fanfare, accompanied by other members of the order, all in ceremonial mantles. The Duchess of Cambridge, wearing a pale yellow coat and carrying a bag made of Strathearn tartan, had taken her seat minutes earlier.

The Dean of the Thistle, the Very Reverend Gilleasbuig Macmillan, conducted the very brief installation ceremony, which took place within the internal Thistle Chapel and was broadcast through speakers to those in the cathedral.

'It is Our pleasure that His Royal Highness The Prince William, Earl of Strathearn be installed a Knight of the Most Ancient and Most Noble Order of the Thistle,' the Queen declared.

The service, which included prayers, readings and hymns, lasted 45 minutes. The choir sang Psalm 122 as the Order of the Thistle procession re-entered the main part of the cathedral and Reverend Macmillan called on the congregation to celebrate 'the leadership the Queen continues to give' in her Diamond Jubilee year. The service concluded with the National Anthem.

A special parade down the Royal Mile to celebrate the Jubilee began shortly afterwards. It featured 400 pipers led by the Lothian and Borders Police Band, which marched from the City Chambers to the Scottish Parliament, opposite the Palace of Holyroodhouse, where folk music, Highland dancing and pipers entertained the crowd.

The royal party, meanwhile, were being given luncheon by the Knights of the Thistle in the Signet Library adjacent to the cathedral.

The Princess Royal and the Earl of Strathearn precede the Queen and the Duke of Edinburgh into St Giles' Cathedral for the Thistle service

OPPOSITE PAGE: The Countess of Strathearn leaves the Signet Library after the luncheon

On the final day of her Diamond Jubilee celebrations in Scotland, the Queen visited Perth. She was handed the keys to the newly dedicated city and her husband was granted the freedom of Perth, which, after a long campaign, had its city status restored as part of a Jubilee competition.

The couple then visited the Black Watch Regimental Museum. The Queen Mother was colonel-in-chief of what is recognised as the best-known Scottish regiment for 65 years until her death in 2002. Her daughter walked through wrought-iron gates commemorating the royal link.

Holyrood Week ended with a civic luncheon at Scone Palace – the ancestral home of the Earls of Mansfield and Mansfield, where Scotland's ancient kings were crowned – and the planting of a tree by the Queen to mark her historic visit.

**FROM FAR LEFT: The Royal Company of Archers provide a guard of honour when the Queen arrives in the city of Perth on 6 July**

**Her Majesty and the Duke of Edinburgh enjoy a performance by the National Youth Pipe Band of Scotland**

**Whilst in Perth the royal couple also visit the Black Watch Regimental Museum at Balhousie Castle**

# July

ONLY DAYS AFTER returning from Scotland, the Queen visited Herefordshire and Worcestershire as part of her Diamond Jubilee tour of the United Kingdom.

Accompanied by the Duke of Edinburgh, the Queen arrived in Hereford by steam train on 11 July and visited the city's 12th-century cathedral. After attending a 'Diamond Day' event at King George V Playing Fields, which included a 90-piece band, a procession of dancers, a cider company's horse-drawn dray and the 2009 Grand National winner, Mon Mome, the royal party was then driven to Worcester.

The Queen officially opened The Hive library and history centre, with the Duke of Gloucester present in his capacity as Chancellor of the University of Worcester. Lunch that day was at the Guildhall, and afterwards the royal couple visited Worcester Cathedral for a special themed service led by the Bishop of Worcester, the Reverend Dr John Inge, to celebrate the area. It included the singing of an excerpt from Tolkien's 'Lord of the Rings' to the music of Elgar's 'Land of Hope and Glory'.

Day two of the West Midlands tour began in Victoria Square in Birmingham, where the Queen and Prince Philip undertook a walkabout and received gifts from city representatives.

The royal party then continued to Queen Elizabeth Hospital Birmingham, where Her Majesty unveiled a piece of glasswork as she officially opened the £545 million building.

**RIGHT: The Prince of Wales and the Duchess of Cornwall join in the fun at a youth rally in Guernsey during their Diamond Jubilee visit to the Channel Islands**

**LEFT: The Queen in Birmingham's Victoria Square on 12 July, the second day of her West Midlands tour**

The hospital is home to the Royal Centre for Defence Medicine, which treats service personnel who are severely wounded overseas. The Queen met past and present patients, volunteers and staff before being presented with a posy by Bethan Davies.

The Queen and the Duke of Edinburgh then flew to the Shropshire Diamond Jubilee Pageant at RAF Cosford. After a reception and luncheon, they took a slow drive around the museum and airfield, and then viewed the pageant in which more than 5,000 children and a number of voluntary groups were taking part.

Next on the royal couple's Diamond Jubilee schedule came North East England, which they visited on 18 and 19 July.

The Queen and Prince Philip arrived at Corporation Quay in Sunderland on the motor yacht *Leander*, having viewed a flypast by a Vulcan bomber that first flew in 1952, the year of Her Majesty's accession. They then toured a Diamond Jubilee exhibition. The royal party were taken to the south side of Tyne Tunnel Two in Jarrow, where the Queen started a wheelchair race and met architects and community leaders before planting a tree.

The royal couple then proceeded to the north side of the tunnel, where Her Majesty gave a speech and unveiled a plaque to mark the official opening of the tunnel.

The Queen and her husband attended a happy (and noisy) Diamond Jubilee celebration in Gateshead International Stadium, where they did a 'driveabout' so that they could be seen by the 8,000 children taking part in a jamboree.

**RIGHT: The Queen tours an exhibition celebrating her 60-year reign at Corporation Quay, Sunderland**

**BELOW: Prince Philip meets Ian 'Spike' Betterton at a reception at the Guildhall in Worcester**

**OPPOSITE PAGE: The royal couple attend the 'Diamond Day' celebrations in Hereford**

After lunching with the Bishop of Durham at Durham Castle, the monarch opened the Queen Elizabeth II Diamond Jubilee White Water Course at the Tees Barrage.

Thousands of people gathered in Leeds the next morning to welcome the Queen and the Duke of Edinburgh. Their tour began at Leeds Arena for a topping-out ceremony before moving on to the renovated City Varieties Music Hall for a 'Good Old Days' performance.

The Queen and Prince Philip started the final day of the regional Diamond Jubilee tour on board *Leander*, placed at their disposal by Sir Donald Gosling. The royal party arrived in Cowes on 25 July through a 'Parade of Sail' while a 21-gun salute was fired from the Royal Yacht Squadron. They alighted at Trinity Landing and walked along the seafront, the Queen stopping to unveil a plaque to mark their visit.

The royal couple also watched a short performance by schoolchildren. They continued on foot to the RNLI lifeboat station, which the Queen formally opened before launching a new lifeboat.

**RIGHT:** The Queen with former prime ministers Sir John Major, Tony Blair and Gordon Brown before a luncheon given by David Cameron at 10 Downing Street

**BELOW:** Her Majesty, having visited the City Varieties Music Hall, walks along Briggate in central Leeds on 19 July

Her Majesty and His Royal Highness went by launch to Cowes Yacht Haven, where they viewed displays by marine volunteer and youth organisations, including the Ellen MacArthur Cancer Trust.

Dame Ellen's charity helps rehabilitate young people after cancer treatment by taking them sailing. 'The Queen was really interested to talk to the young men and women, and was totally engaged and interested in what we do,' she said.

The royal couple left the Isle of Wight by helicopter and were flown to the New Forest Agricultural Showground near Brockenhurst in Hampshire, where they were met by the show's president, Alan Titchmarsh, before touring the packed showground by car and on foot.

That afternoon, the Queen and the Duke of Edinburgh were shown livestock and presented prizes. They also visited the 'Best of British Marquee' and inspected local produce before leaving for Windsor.

And that was it: after more than 80 engagements around the United Kingdom, the seemingly indefatigable royal couple's Diamond Jubilee tour, which had begun in Leicester more than four months earlier, had come to an end.

**OPPOSITE PAGE: The Queen with the crew of Cowes RNLI lifeboat station during her Diamond Jubilee visit to the Isle of Wight on 25 July**

**BELOW: As the sun shines, Her Majesty is clearly enjoying the last day of her action-packed, four-month tour of the United Kingdom**

**The Duke of Edinburgh, pictured visiting the New Forest Agricultural Showground, is in equally good form after a health scare the previous month**

The Duke and Duchess of Cambridge, both dressed in brightly coloured grass skirts, dance the night away in the South Seas

# Flying Visits

## By RICHARD PALMER

IT WAS HARD to imagine a better trip than the one they enjoyed in Canada and California, but the Duke and Duchess of Cambridge's Asia-Pacific tour was manna from heaven for royal watchers. William and Kate's second overseas tour, after their official visit to North America last year, had everything: glamour, controversy, exotic photographs, a dancing duchess, and the sight of the future King and his wife stepping up a gear and taking on new responsibilities on behalf of the Queen.

It was enough to make some of the photographers, often quick to see the negative side, positively ecstatic. 'We've waited 20 years for these sorts of pictures. We won't see the likes of this again,' said one exhausted, sweaty but happy snapper, a veteran of the Diana days, sitting in a tropical hotel bar at the end of the tour. 'It's all downhill from here.'

Not necessarily where this couple are concerned. The royal story, stagnant for so long, has taken off since they got engaged two years ago and who can say where it will lead?

Their visit to Singapore, Malaysia, the Solomon Islands and Tuvalu was on behalf of the Queen to celebrate her Diamond Jubilee in the four Commonwealth countries, the last two of which are proud to count the monarch as their head of state.

Befitting such a celebration, there were smiles aplenty but also a more formal, grown-up series of engagements than on their first tour last year. And then, mid-way through the nine-day trip, came news that the Duchess had been photographed topless while sunbathing on a brief holiday in southern France a few days earlier.

The resulting controversy cast a shadow over the rest of the tour, although after the shock and anger had worn off, the couple put on a brave face and smiled their way through it.

In Singapore, they began with a poignant tribute to William's mother by inspecting a flower planted in her honour three weeks after her death. Diana, Princess of Wales, had been due to visit the city-state in September 1997 and view her white orchid at the National Botanic Gardens, but her death in a Paris car crash the previous month meant she never got to see it. Looking at the *Dendrobium* 'Memoria Princess Diana', a sombre William said: 'It's beautiful, beautiful. That's very nice.'

Naming orchids after prominent visitors is a Singapore tradition and the Cambridges were shown *Vanda* 'William Catherine', a purple and white one planted in their honour, as well as one named after the Queen in 1972. In a nod to her hosts, Kate wore a Jenny Packham-designed kimono-style pink dress with an orchid pattern.

The royal couple, who stayed in a luxury suite amid the colonial splendour of Raffles Hotel, were later given a guard of honour welcome at the Istana, the official residence of President Tony Tan Keng Yam, before attending a glittering state banquet.

With Kate dazzling in a £710 purple and white floral patterned dress by Singapore-born designer Prabal Gurung, they dined on a seven-course Chinese meal and the Duke paid tribute to the historic ties between Britain and its former colony, which won independence in 1965.

The next morning came one of those glorious moments that reporters dream about. On a noisy walkabout among fans chanting 'Will, you're brill; Kate, you're great', someone decided to ask William how many children he and his wife wanted. 'Two,' he replied, in a rare unguarded moment.

Or at least we think he did. If truth be told it was hearsay. A girl in the crowd said she had heard him say it to a little boy but nobody could trace him.

In any case, the story, never denied, went around the world. It was thought to be the first time that either William or Kate had put a figure publicly on the number of offspring they would like.

In 33C heat and high humidity, the sweat was pouring off Prince William; some in the 1,000-strong crowd fainted during their three-hour wait to see the couple.

Kate, wearing a white broderie anglaise suit by Alexander McQueen, was spotted holding a packet of antiseptic wipes, almost hidden beneath her clutchbag, after shaking hands with so many enthusiastic fans.

At a new £350 million Rolls-Royce factory, where the Duchess was photographed for the first time wearing wraparound safety goggles, the couple flew the flag for UK business.

It was quickly emerging that this was a tour that in most parts could equally have been done by William's grandparents or father and stepmother.

A senior royal aide acknowledged the new seriousness after the fun and informality of their trip to Canada and the United States and their determination to take on more heavyweight engagements.

**LEFT: The Duke and Duchess attend a state dinner given by President Tony Tan Keng Yam and his wife at the Istana**

**FROM FAR LEFT: The royal couple admire the *Vanda* 'William Catherine' orchid named in their honour at the Botanic Gardens**

**They are also shown the *Dendrobium* 'Memoria Princess Diana' orchid created when William's mother was still alive**

'It's certainly something they're very aware of. They want to do the job seriously and do it commensurate with their age and status,' he said.

The next morning, the Duchess, in a bespoke Jenny Packham duck egg blue dress, sheltered from the blistering sun beneath a parasol and joined William at a moving ceremony in Kranji Cemetery to pay tribute to 24,000 war dead.

They then flew to the Malaysian capital, Kuala Lumpur, where Kate notched up another milestone, making her first overseas speech, during a heart-rending visit to dying and seriously ill children at a hospice.

Her speech was a more accomplished performance than her first, rather nervous, effort at a hospice in Ipswich in March, but what was perhaps more memorable was the way she lit up the day for the young patients at Hospis Malaysia, many of whom had been listless until she arrived.

Among them was Zakwan Anuar, 15, a very sick leukaemia patient who had postponed a blood transfusion to see her and awoke to tell the Duchess she was 'very pretty'.

'Thank you. You're very handsome,' replied Kate, who also told him he was 'very, very brave'.

His tearful mother, Norizan Sulong, had worried he would not survive long enough to meet the Duchess.

'It was as if the leukaemia had gone,' she said. 'I thought I had lost him. He doesn't have long.' Sadly, Zakwan died two weeks later.

That night the Duchess of Cambridge glittered in an exquisitely embroidered floor-length bespoke Alexander McQueen dress at a state dinner given by the Yang di-Pertuan Agong – the King of Malaysia – and his wife at the opulent new Istana Negara palace in Kuala Lumpur.

Kate awoke next morning to a crisis. Grim-faced courtiers, roused at 5am to be told of French *Closer* magazine's plan to publish topless photographs of her, briefed the couple over breakfast at the British High Commission. Pity the poor aides who had to tell them.

It was the Duchess's misfortune that news of the embarrassing photographs broke on the morning that she and William were visiting a mosque for the first time, a landmark for a future king and queen who will have millions of Muslim subjects in Britain and around the Commonwealth.

**RIGHT: Protective eyewear is required when the couple tour the Rolls-Royce factory in Singapore**

**OPPOSITE PAGE: Kate meets Zakwan Anuar and his mother at Hospis Malaysia in Kuala Lumpur**

**BELOW: The Cambridges pay a poignant visit to Kranji War Cemetery before leaving Singapore**

Kate, wrapped in a headscarf and dressed demurely in a matching grey Beulah dress, inevitably evoked comparisons with Diana as she toured the mosque in her stocking feet, asking numerous questions about Islam.

Always self-composed in public, she smiled her way through it as the world's cameras focused on her, looking for signs of stress and upset. Behind the scenes, aides told how the couple were 'hurt, shocked, furious and disgusted' and drew comparisons with the treatment meted out to William's mother.

He was less able to keep a check on his emotions, stomping head down, jaw clenched to a plane for Borneo despite Kate's pleading to put on a show and smile for the cameras.

Her steeliness and grace under pressure won plaudits from veteran royal watchers who saw in her another strong Windsor woman to follow Queen Mary, Queen Elizabeth the Queen Mother and Queen Elizabeth II.

In the Malaysian state of Sabah, on Borneo, she and William were hoisted up 130ft to explore the rainforest on a rope canopy walkway before flying the next day to the Solomon Islands and its capital, Honiara, on Guadalcanal.

In the former British protectorate, they were given a spectacular South Pacific welcome by warriors in loincloths and grass skirts when they landed in a charter plane.

They received a traditional challenge, a *tuku baka* – the Solomon Islands' equivalent of a Maori *haka* – by tribal elders and warriors brandishing spears, axes, bows and slingshots as drummers pounded out a beat.

**RIGHT: The Duke and Duchess walk through the rainforest at Danum Valley research centre in Sabah**

**OPPOSITE PAGE FROM FAR LEFT: William and Kate attend the dinner given by the King and Queen of Malaysia**

**In keeping with Muslim tradition the Duchess of Cambridge ensures that her head is covered at Assyakirin Mosque**

**A lighter moment as the royal couple prepare to enter the Kuala Lumpur mosque**

Father Henry Teho, an Anglican priest and tribal elder wearing a traditional mat skirt made from grass, tree bark and pandanus leaves, explained: 'When you used to come to the Solomon Islands it was a challenge that we'll kill you and eat you but now it's just a challenge saying you are from a different culture.'

'We are very honoured to be greeting the Prince. We just heard about Kate when she got married to the Prince. She is the chosen one. That makes her very important.'

Police estimated more than 70,000 people, the largest turnout of the tour, lined the five-mile route from the airport to Honiara to greet the royal couple as they drove by on a carnival-style float, a flat-bed Toyota truck decorated as a war canoe.

That evening, at an outdoor state banquet, the couple accidentally committed a diplomatic gaffe when they wore what they thought were traditional brightly coloured Solomon Islands outfits left by their hosts in their hotel bedroom. Unfortunately, it transpired they were actually presents for them from a designer based in the Cook Islands, 2,762 miles away. The argument over who was to blame for the mix-up was still ongoing 10 days later.

In Honiara on their second day, the Duchess, wearing a yellow Jaeger dress, was hailed as an island princess when she was crowned unexpectedly with a floral headdress made from exotic frangipani and bougainvillea.

Everywhere she looked that day, there were bare-breasted maidens, a potentially tricky photo opportunity as the topless pictures row rumbled on, but the Duchess continued as if she were meeting Knightsbridge ladies in twin sets and pearls.

In the evening though came blessed relief: a romantic getaway to a paradise island, where the couple were able to enjoy a few hours of down time in a £780-a-night secluded thatched leaf bungalow away from the cameras.

**FROM FAR LEFT: The Duke and Duchess of Cambridge travel to the cathedral in Honiara on a *tomoko* (war canoe) mounted on a white truck**

**Kate tours a cultural village and is pleased to receive a wood carving of a canoe from one of the younger residents**

**The couple are traditionally dressed for a Solomon Islands state dinner; it transpired that their outfits were made thousands of miles away**

The royal visitors are carried from a boat to their plane in Marau, Solomon Islands, on 18 September

LEFT: William and Kate are barefoot when they arrive at the private island resort of Tavanipupu

Prince William uses a machete to
open a coconut from a tree planted
by the Queen 30 years earlier

OPPOSITE PAGE: The Duke and
Duchess attend an Island Dinner
at Tausoa Lima Falekaupule

They travelled to the private island resort of Tavanipupu, a former coconut plantation, in an ornately-decorated dugout war canoe escorted by warriors. Alongside them were men swimming inside wire-framed replicas of sharks, long worshipped in the islands and whose spirits were traditionally evoked on raiding parties.

Once the cameras had gone, the couple went snorkelling in the idyllic Marau Sound lagoon and sat eating dinner on their own private jetty in a tropical downpour. Pamela Kimberly, the resort's co-owner, said: 'I was astounded at how down to earth and lovely they were. They seemed to love it. They were happy and relaxed.'

William and Kate returned to the capital the next morning and, after a brief farewell at the airport, flew on to their final destination, the tiny island nation of Tuvalu.

They were carried shoulder high off their plane on a double throne by 25 grass-skirted men when they arrived on Funafuti, Tuvalu's main island. At least half of the population turned out to greet them in a ceremony echoing the welcome given to the Queen and the Duke of Edinburgh at the start of Tuvalu's previous royal visit in 1982, when warriors transported them from the royal yacht *Britannia* in canoes.

Inside a hall, William and Kate were honoured with a rousing tribal welcome. Crown garlands of frangipani flowers were placed on their heads during what is known as a *falekaupule* ceremony.

'*Talofa*' – 'Hello,' said William, before recalling that iconic reception given to his grandmother 30 years ago.

'It is the highlight of the Diamond Jubilee tour on her behalf. We are delighted to be here. Your wonderful welcome has to be the most original and quite literally uplifting ever. We will both remember it and the joy and happiness of what has followed for the rest of our lives.'

It got even better. That night we were treated to images of a dancing duke and duchess. It was 'some enchanted evening' indeed for the second-in-line to the throne and his wife as they danced in colourful grass skirts to the sounds of the South Pacific.

With skirts made from pandanus leaves tied over their outfits, William and his dancing queen shimmied and swayed their hips as they joined six communities at a *fatele* party where groups try to out-sing or out-dance each other.

Time after time, Kate, wearing an Alice Temperley dress beneath her grass skirt, got to her feet to join the performers. William cooled his wife with a fan but left it late to try out his moves. When they danced together, they could not stop laughing, liberally sprinkling a bottle of Paul Smith London eau de toilette for men over performers in keeping with the tradition for dignitaries to spray perfume on the dancers.

Asked how it had gone, William replied: 'Good, really good – an amazing evening.'

They stayed overnight in an apartment loaned to them by an Australian naval officer away on leave and left the next day carried aloft again by islanders. It was perhaps rather fitting that after the low point of the topless photos episode they ended the tour as they began it: on a high.

The incredible scene as the Duke and Duchess of Cambridge are carried to their plane by Tuvalu Islanders

OPPOSITE PAGE: 'Cathleen' uses a new fan to counteract the heat of the South Pacific evening

# Autumn

W HILST STILL ON holiday in Scotland, the Queen unveiled a plaque marking a special Diamond Jubilee cairn close to her Balmoral estate. The residents of Ballater, Aberdeenshire, had collected 60 stones from hills in the surrounding area to create the display.

During a late-afternoon visit to the village, the Queen met Gordon Bruce and Alistair Cassie, who came up with the idea for the commemorative work.

Mr Bruce, a retired builder, said: 'We felt the royalty had done a lot for Ballater and we should do something for the Jubilee. We got permission to go on all the estates to collect the stones. The blacksmith and so on has done everything for nothing – the community spirit has been great.'

The Queen walked along the main street, which had been decorated with flags. The crowd cheered and applauded as she reached the green near the church, where children lifted a cover of Balmoral tartan to reveal the cairn.

The largest stone is inscribed 'Queen Elizabeth II' and '1952 Jubilee 2012'. The smaller stones are set within a bed of mixed heather next to a plaque listing the 30 hills from which they came.

Her Majesty met residents of the village before leaving along a route lined with flaming torches in the same way that Queen Victoria left the village during her Diamond Jubilee in 1897.

The day after she returned south, the Queen unveiled an artwork in Windsor to mark her Diamond Jubilee.

**LEFT: The Queen walks through the village of Ballater in Aberdeenshire before the unveiling of the Diamond Jubilee tribute**

**RIGHT: Her Majesty talks to Gordon Bruce as local children Elise Smith, 8, and Jack O'Halloran, 9, uncover the impressive cairn**

The spiral of 60 spheres – 59 made from polished stainless steel and one cut-glass sphere at the top – has been installed by the Windsor and Eton Society on the concourse in King Edward Court shopping centre. It was designed by Caroline Basra, 15, a pupil at Windsor Girls' School, who won a competition to design an appropriate Jubilee tribute.

'I can't believe it,' said the Year 11 pupil. 'I am so glad that she was able to come and unveil it.'

The Queen asked Caroline if she was considering becoming an artist and she replied that she had not yet decided, although she is currently studying GCSE art.

A week later, some of those who worked on the celebrations for Her Majesty's Diamond Jubilee year attended a reception hosted by the Queen and Duke of Edinburgh at Buckingham Palace. Among the 350 guests on 16 October were singer Gary Barlow and chef Heston Blumenthal.

Barlow organised the Diamond Jubilee Concert in June, and was later awarded an OBE for services to the entertainment industry and to charity.

'I just thought the event deserved such notice from everybody and I think everybody was so proud that the Queen had made it to this point and the amazing job she has done for so long for us all,' he said. 'We were all proud to be a part of it.'

The Marquess of Salisbury, one of the senior organisers of the Thames Diamond Jubilee Pageant and chairman of the Thames Diamond Jubilee Foundation, also attended the reception.

'I thought it was a triumph, the whole thing – I thought the country took a look at itself and rather liked what it saw,' said Lord Salisbury.

'It was nice because it wasn't triumphalist, and there was an element of surprise about it. What I liked about it was [people] understood the Queen embodied the nation. That's what she does.'

**ABOVE:** The Queen hosts a reception for organisers and supporters of the Diamond Jubilee celebrations at Buckingham Palace on 16 October

**LEFT:** Princess Anne with a Duke of Edinburgh International Award winner in Lusaka during her Diamond Jubilee tour of Zambia in September

**OPPOSITE PAGE:** Her Majesty stands in front of the Windsor and Eton Society Diamond Jubilee tribute on 9 October

Watched by a large crowd at the King Edward Court shopping centre, the monarch unveils the striking artwork which marks her 60-year reign

The Duke of Kent visits the Uganda Rapid Deployment Centre and UPDF Senior Command and Staff College at Jinja during his Diamond Jubilee tour

# Acknowledgments

I would like to thank Lynne Bell, Richard Palmer, Ingrid Seward and Camilla Tominey for their invaluable contributions to *Jubilee 2012: Celebrations & Tours*.

Once again I am grateful to Darren Reeve for his time and patience while this book was being designed.

I must also thank Sarah Hill at Press Association Images for all her help with this project.

Joe Little
Managing Editor, *Majesty* magazine

London, October 2012